Tracking the signifier

Theoretical essays:
film, linguistics, literature

In memory of my father

Nunc mea Pierios cupiam per pectora fontes
Irriguas torquere vias, totumque per ora
Volvere laxatum gemino de vertice rivum;
Ut, tenues oblita sonos, audacibus alis
Surgat in officium venerandi Musa parentis.
Hoc utcunque tibi gratum, pater optime, carmen
Exiguum meditatur opus, nec novimus ipsi
Aptius a nobis quae possint munera donis
Respondere tuis, quamvis nec maxima possint
Respondere tuis, nedum ut par gratia donis
Esse queat, vacuis quae redditur arida verbis.

John Milton

Tracking the signifier

Theoretical essays:
film, linguistics, literature

COLIN MacCABE

University of Minnesota Press, Minneapolis

Copyright © Colin MacCabe 1985

Published in the USA by the University of Minnesota Press
2037 University Avenue
Southeast, Minneapolis
MN 55414

Library of Congress cataloging in publication data

Applied for. *Number:* 85-51114

ISBN 0 8166 1460 1 *cased*
0 8166 1462 8 *paper*

Printed in the United Kingdom

Contents

Provenance of the essays
and acknowledgements

Class of '68: Elements of an intellectual autobiography 1967–1981' is here published for the first time.

'Realism and the cinema: Notes on some Brechtian theses' first appeared in *Screen* 15, 2, summer 1974.

'Theory and film: principles of realism and pleasure' was given in slightly different forms to a SEFT weekend school and to the Literature and Theory conference at Essex in 1976. First published in *Screen* 17, 3, autumn 1976.

'On discourse' was originally the opening seminar in a course on 'Discourse and Social Relations' organised by Paul Hirst and Sami Zubaida at Birkbeck College, London in October 1976. It was reworked for a seminar on psychoanalysis and language which I organised at King's College, Cambridge in 1978 and published in a collection which I edited from that seminar entitled *The Talking Cure: Essays in Psychoanalysis and Language*. It is here reprinted by permission of the Macmillan Press.

'Language, linguistics and the study of literature' was first presented to the Cambridge Linguistics Society in the summer of 1979 and a revised version was given as a lecture to the Oxford University English Faculty in the same term. It was first published in the *Oxford Literary Review*, 4, 3, summer 1981.

'Realism: Balzac and Barthes' was a contribution to Cambridge University French department's research seminar in February 1983. It was reworked for my own research seminar at Strathclyde University and reached final form in July 1983 in Urbana-Champaign at a conference organised by the University of Illinois entitled 'Marxism and the interpretation of culture'. It is also published in the proceedings of that conference.

Preface

Much of what might be said in a preface takes up the substance of the introductory essay.

I have been very fortunate in twice belonging to quite exceptional groupings where I found the energy and excitement which should always accompany intellectual work but so rarely does.

I should like to record my thanks to Sam Rohdie who asked me onto the *Screen* editorial board and to all the then members of that board from whom I learned so much, even in disagreement: Ben Brewster, Ed Buscombe, Elizabeth Cowie, Christine Gledhill, Kari Hanet, John Halliday, Stephen Heath, Jim Hillier, Alan Lovell, Paul Willemen, Christopher Williams, Peter Wollen.

At King's my colleagues were friends but their friendship never prevented them from teaching me a thing or two, frequently. Thanks, and more, to John Barrell, Norman Bryson, Frank Kermode, Dadie Rylands, David Simpson and Tony Tanner.

In addition I must specially thank Stephen Heath, a friend in every adversity, Jocelyn Cornwell, who always provided a fresh intellectual perspective, but above all, in the context of these essays, Ben Brewster, who taught me all I know about film and most of what I know about linguistics.

The introductory essay runs the inevitable risk of any biography however tentative or partial: a coherence always more retrospective than willed, an importance for the protagonist more narrative than historical. But to these general reservations one must add more local ones. In focusing on the institutional settings of intellectual debates, those debates are inevitably overspecified. It is not simply that most of the crucial moments and

Preface

presences in one's life are missing. The impact of contemporary presences in one's life are missing. The impact of contemporary novels and poetry, of our current sounds and images is unrelated because unresolved. And this is perhaps inevitable with the choice of subject and form. As a result what can be specified and understood is given precedence over that which is still at work, still partially unconscious. Thus, feminism which produced many of the concerns and emphases for the work collected here is curiously unimportant for an account which focuses on definable intellectual institutions. But the paradox is largely apparent because feminism cannot be located as such a definable institution: to specify it in terms of ideas *or* politics *or* its impact on everyday life is to reduce the importance of a movement across all these levels. To capture such a movement would require a different kind of writing.

Perhaps that is just another way of indicating the major problem of an introduction that in its very form and language presupposes an importance for theoretical reflection that is questioned at the level of content. But to find a way of writing which would stress both the importance and unimportance of theory is a dilemma that has repeated itself in western culture since Nietzsche. It is only at some vanishing point in the future where the division between mental and manual labour is less insistent that this dilemma may finally dissolve itself.

Strathclyde University 9 October 1984

Class of '68: elements of an intellectual autobiography 1967–81

I can still remember with all the clarity that normally attaches to screen memories, the shock I received when I first read the introduction to Roland Barthes's *Essais Critiques*, a collection of his occasional criticism which had been published five years earlier in 1964. I think that I had hoped that the introduction, by tying together essays from a period of a decade, would explain to me the unworried inconsistency which seemed to mark Barthes's work, especially when he was pledged, in the late sixties, to a consistent reading of literature. I suppose also that I wished to get a firmer fix on this anonymous figure who wrote so personally about the impersonal. It was with some such expectations that I turned to the introduction. But Barthes refused to introduce his essays. To write was to give up all rights, the text was left for others as the writer became simply another reader, unable to guarantee the true meanings of his or her own texts, or providing such a guarantee only at the risk of a bad faith which tried to freeze meanings in memory. Barthes's refusal of a canonical meaning for his own texts and the consequent ethic of a fundamental discontinuity of meaning and self appeared as a threat – do I not even possess my own meanings, do I not even possess an 'I' – but also as a surmise – and what would it be like to live under that sign?

That introduction crystallised for me much of what at that period, both before that frozen moment in the library and after, was so seductive about the explosion of work that erupted out of Paris in the middle and late sixties. And this emphasis on discontinuity, on heterogeneity, on the falseness of identities both semantic and social seemed to figure at the intellectual level the more pressing truths that were offered by the experiences of the late sixties when the revolution and the counter-culture promised in evanescent moments to be one and the same. The standard articulation of those experiences was, however, in the heavy and normative tones of an existentialism or a Marxism which tried to produce a unity of consciousness, where, it is ever more clear in retrospect, what was being celebrated was the possibility of a diversity of experience which could only be collapsed together at the cost of madness or morality. The importance of the sixties is not to be located in some mythical moment in the past where a specious unity was possible, but in the investigation of methods of articulating the differences of late capitalist societies that might yet help us to realise the possibility of a genuine plurality way beyond what can be imagined within the ideology of pluralism of discrete interests which our western societies offer as models for both personal and political development.

Re-reading Barthes's essay today, what strikes me is the extent to which Barthes remains attached to a realm of the personal untouched by the differentiation of language and the social; how the investigation of the sociality of language is premissed on an area of the private which is absolute. At the end of a discussion about the dialectic between 'originality' and 'banality' Barthes continues: 'Whoever wants to write with exactitude must therefore proceed to the frontiers of language, and it is in this that he actually writes *for others* (if he spoke only to himself, a kind of spontaneous nomenclature of his feelings would suffice, for feeling is immediately its own name)'.[1] Barthes here draws back from a more radical thought: even our most intimate feelings can only be named socially because, outside of the public form of a language, we would have no criteria whereby we could recognise the same emotion as the same. Barthes's spontaneous nomenclature is none other than the belief in a secret naming that Wittgenstein took such pains to show was self-contradictory – there are no private languages. And if Barthes retained at the heart of his project an area of the private which finally, in his last and most moving book, he turned to systematise, he also retains its inevitable analogue, a public world which is undifferentiated except for the fact of its 'publicity'. Barthes refuses to consider his essays in terms of a necessarily delusive personal coherence, but he also

2

refuses to consider them in terms of the various institutional battles and struggles in which they were produced.

In introducing these essays I have no desire to try and make them finally coherent, to avoid all possible mis-readings both past and future by producing a reading now which would cancel all previous readings (including my own) and petrify the results under my control. The egocentric task does not appeal, or rather, its appeal is undercut by the knowledge of its impossibility. There is, however, a different desire in this introduction – the possibility of situating these essays, of describing the specific struggles and institutions which constituted the context if not the meaning of these texts. To undertake such a situation seems of value to me today as a method, at least personal, of marking the end of a particular period. If the publication of a selection of essays inevitably relates to financial and career motives which should not be underestimated simply because they are so little discussed, such considerations could not alone justify the painful task of collecting and reconsidering material which seemed consigned to the past.

Such a reconsideration seems necessary as part of a re-evaluation of the confident appeal to the rigour of theory which was such a striking feature of the late sixties and their immediate aftermath. For those engaged in the analysis of texts (and if that word immediately suggested literary texts at the beginning of the seventies, it was as likely to refer to film and television at the end) there was a renewed interest in the formal analyses of language, in psychoanalysis and in the possibilities of Marxism. If it may be analytically clearer and pedagogically more useful to divide these strands up and attach convenient labels and names to them, it is important to remember that these three elements were seen as part of a single effort, a determination to produce an understanding of texts which would be adequate to their reality and specificity but which would relate them to wider political and cultural struggles. The aim was nothing less than an understanding of the functionings of language and culture. The unity of the theoretical project was underpinned by a political over-valuation of theory which was one of the products of the political movements of the late sixties. This over-valuation often depended on a confident running together of the domains of politics, education and culture in over-simplified ways, but that over-simplification and that confidence were not without their positive aspects.

Theoretical essays

London: Screen

Throughout the seventies in Britain, the most important consistent attempts to discuss and analyse the relations between culture and signification took place in the pages of the film magazine, *Screen*. And it is hardly accidental that the *Screen* of the seventies was itself a product of the political movements of the late sixties. Originally both *Screen* and its parent body SEFT (Society for Education in Film and Television) were set up at the end of the fifties by teachers interested in bringing film into the classroom, and it was practical questions about the teaching of film which dominated the magazine for its first twelve years. Throughout this period both the society and the magazine were located within the offices of the British Film Institute, which was the society's funding body.

Screen's transformation into a theoretical magazine is a complicated and complex history. At the intellectual level, however, the problems of reconciling film with traditional conceptions of art made a theoretical magazine a pressing necessity for teachers. Unfortunately the easiest way for teachers to argue for film within the school was to stress film as a great new artistic medium. If its commercialisation in the States had not allowed the artistic potential to develop, the argument continued, in Europe there was a long tradition of particularly gifted individuals who had transferred their personal vision of the world onto celluloid. The problem with such an argument for many teachers was that it reproduced exactly the traditional romantic valuation of art as the product of a superior individual consciousness and denigrated film in so far as it was part of a popular culture. The teachers who were introducing film into the schools were often those most influenced by writers such as Hoggart, Williams and Hall who argued against traditional conceptions of art and in favour of a serious consideration of the forms and values of popular culture. And to give that ideological position a pedagogic edge, the films that many teachers most wanted to discuss with their pupils were the intellectually despised products of Hollywood. This particular contradiction gained a further dialectical twist throughout the sixties as the theses and theories of *Cahiers du Cinéma* gained ground in the English-speaking world. *Cahiers*, probably the most influential post-war cultural magazine in the west, had argued for a new valuation of Hollywood by concentrating on those

4

directors who it considered managed to mark their films with a personal style and thus deserved the culturally privileged status of an *auteur*. The paradox of the *Cahiers* position was that it offered a powerful intellectual defence of Hollywood, and that in its pages it provided a great deal of material for teachers, but that this defence and this material was dependent on a concept of the artist drawn from traditional aesthetics. The popular culture of Hollywood was transformed to reveal the high art of the *Cahiers*-selected *auteur*.

Many of the most vital and important debates about education and culture were thus a matter of daily reality for anybody interested in teaching film. It is thus not surprising that 1968 was to affect this group of teachers with considerable force. I use that particular date simply as a convenient shorthand for that movement in the late sixties which placed questions about education, culture and lifestyle at the centre of a political agenda drawn up in schools and universities throughout the world. Régis Debray intended to mock the pretentions of that time when he said of the French students that in 1968 they had set out on a voyage to China and ended up on the shores of California. The jibe can be read against its intentions to reveal some measure of the intercontinental complexity of a movement whose effects as felt within feminism and the ecological movement provide the most vital political forces in the developed world and whose potential is still the only hope for a revitalisation and redefinition of a socialist project for society.

Specifically, in the more parochial context of the BFI and SEFT, the political rupture came in 1971 with the resignation of Paddy Whannel, head of the BFI education department, together with five members of his staff. The fundamental dispute which underlay these resignations was the demand by Whannel and the Education Department that the BFI should adopt an active educational policy which would seek to influence subject matter and method in film education rather than simply responding to specific requests from teachers. In some senses the Education Department was asking the BFI to undertake a task which the universities were manifestly ill-equipped to contemplate, partly because of their ignorance of film and partly because of their commitment to traditional cultural values, these two factors being intimately related. Behind the education department's

5

demand was a widespread feeling that the rebirth of Marxist theory and the new wave of interest in formalist studies, particularly in France, offered a genuine possibility of analysing film in ways which would avoid the traditional cultural assumptions of *auteur* theory. The aim was nothing less than to constitute film as a rigorous object of study and the implied consequence, conscious or not, was a redrawing of both object and method in the humanities. If the resignations were the signal of a lost battle within the BFI, the war continued as the BFI, in recognition of the importance of a new educational policy, made a hugely increased grant to SEFT which became a genuinely autonomous body. Symbolically SEFT moved out of the BFI's offices and started its new role by reconstituting *Screen* as a magazine which would provide a focus for theoretical debates about film. It is vital, when considering the history of *Screen* in the seventies, to remember this unparalleled material and educational base which sharply differentiates *Screen* from many other contemporary radical intellectual magazines. To dispose of sufficient funds to run a proper office with a staff of three or four meant that the magazine was liberated from the constant worry of where the money or time was going to come for the next issue. This strong material base was the product of a genuine series of needs within education and the particular struggle that had been waged with the BFI.

Screen was thus ideally placed to undertake fresh work in cultural analysis. For subject-matter it had the great popular art of the twentieth century, virtually untouched by academic analysis, and for method it could draw on a whole series of arguments about culture and politics that had flourished in the twenties and early thirties but which had received little further attention until they resurfaced with fresh inflections and new emphases in France in the sixties. For the lazy and the professionally ignorant, and they are legion, such work is, unbelievably, still characterised as structuralist. The particular features of structuralist analysis, however, play only a small part in a more general movement which sought to understand cultural processes as systems of signification. The use of linguistics as a model to study these systems led to enormous gains at the level of the specificity of the analyses, but more important was the attempt to link questions of signification to questions of subjectivity. It was around signification and subjectivity that this new work connected to Marxism. Marxism's abiding problem has always been to explain the way in which capitalist relations reproduce themsclvcs in non-coercive ways. Throughout the seventies there were many who felt that the key to such an understanding lay in an analysis of culture which would not simply read it off as an effect of the economic base but would understand its ability to reproduce subjectivities, a reproduction finally determined by the economic relations but the mechanisms of which had to be comprehended in their own right.

In the first years, from 1971–3, *Screen*'s major effort was to present and produce material that was not widely available in Britain. Material from the twenties and thirties drawn from the Russian Formalists and Benjamin was juxtaposed with recent French work from *Cahiers du Cinéma* and *Cinéthique*. This work drew on Christian Metz's semiology of the cinema but criticised a simple descriptive semiology from a Marxist viewpoint much influenced by Lacanian psychoanalysis. It was in the context of this conjunction of semiology with Marxism and psychoanalysis that Kari Hanet, Stephen Heath and myself joined the board of the magazine in the summer of 1973. Stephen Heath and I had already collaborated for some time. In 1971, in my final year as an undergraduate at Cambridge, we had, together with Christopher Prendergast, published a small volume of essays entitled *Signs of the Times: Introductory Readings in Textual Semiotics*. The book had its origin in an article by Julia Kristeva on semiotics which Stephen Heath and Chris Prendergast had translated and which subsequently had been refused publication. I had been editing *Granta*, a student magazine, throughout the year and, carried away by enthusiasm, we suddenly found ourselves producing and printing a small book which laid out much of the current thinking of Derrida, Barthes and the *Tel Quel* group. Since that time I had started work on a thesis on Joyce's language and spent a year in Paris studying at the Ecole Normale Supérieure where I attended Althusser's and Derrida's classes. The summer of 1973 saw me back in England and the possibility of working on the cinema was immensely exciting. On the one hand Cambridge seemed an intellectual desert and, on the other, the cinema offered a peculiarly appropriate field for confronting some of the problems of the ultra-modernist positions adopted by Barthes and the *Tel Quel* group. If their analyses of the classic texts of French modernism, Mallarmé, Bataille, Artaud, were intellectually compelling and enabled a reading of Joyce and Pound which broke with the sterility of Leavis's restriction of modernism to Lawrence and Eliot, the political weight given to writing which disrupted the stability of meaning and identity was deeply problematic. If questions of subjectivity were placed at the centre of political inquiry, the only politically valid form of art was one which broke with any fixity of meaning to inaugurate a new decentred form of being. Such a position ignored totally the vast popular forms of film and television, reducing them to mere agencies of the reproduction of a fixed and fixated subjectivity condemned to endlessly consume the meanings and identities produced for it. This position foreclosed any encounter with or differentiation of the vast reality of popular culture, seeking salvation in a generalisation of the explosive force that modernism represented to traditional high culture. It further denied any interest in the dominant left political traditions which had valued art in general, and film in particular, in relation to canons of realism. The first two articles in this collection, and indeed all of my work for *Screen* circulated around these problems. It was the juxtaposition of Brecht and psychoanalysis, a juxtaposition largely encouraged by work on *Screen*, which provided for me some possible resolutions of these problems, linking the advances of the French theorists to a more useful political account of culture, providing a new way of thinking through the relationship between the social and the individual.

The psychoanalysis appealed to was the reading of Freud elaborated by the French psychoanalyst Jacques Lacan. Lacan's theory emphasised that the unconscious was the product of the body's entry into a signifying system which was always unstable, never finished. The ego was an imaginary production forged and re-forged by the attempt to stabilise both subject and meaning, while the unconscious was the product of the fact that meaning could not be so stabilised. The advantage of Lacan over other versions of psychoanalysis was that the text, whether literary or filmic, ceased to be the representation of the author's psychic conflict but became the enactment of a series of conflicts shared by author and reader. The text was thus granted a reality but at the risk that all texts became versions of the same basic psychic conflict. If the Oedipus complex as a series of biographical struggles within the family was replaced by the Oedipus complex as a structure which revealed the impossibility of mastering one's own meaning, the majority of texts became inevitable failures to affirm an intelligibility that they couldn't possess. All attempts at meaning became so many unworthy lures which attempted to seal the subject into an imaginary position of closure. Lacanian psychoanalysis, thus used by the *Tel Quel* group, furnished a criterion of value – insofar as the text remained open so did the subject. And it was this subject in process, never arrested within a fixed identity, which functioned as a new political model of subjectivity, the final break with a bourgeois ideology understood largely as an ideology of closure and identity.

The specificity of film was to be located in the field of vision: insofar as a film fixed the subject in a position of imaginary dominance through the security of vision then it fell immediately within bourgeois ideology, insofar as it broke that security it offered fresh possibilities. It was by drawing on psychoanalytic accounts of vision in voyeurism and fetishism that *Screen* elaborated its account and critique of the cinema. The disruption of the imaginary security of the ego by a problematising of vision was linked to Brecht's emphasis on the breaking of the identificatory processes in the theatre as the precondition for the production of political knowledge. To characterise *Screen* in the period 1974–6 in terms of Brecht and psychoanalysis is to reduce the variety and fertility of the work carried out in that period. The whole effort to understand the mechanisms of identification and representation at work in film went well beyond any simple conjunction of Brecht and psychoanalysis, and from an abundance of genuinely original work one might single out Stephen Heath's attempt to develop adequate terms for the analysis of film and Laura Mulvey's theorisation of visual pleasure from a feminist perspective. Nevertheless, all that work, as well as the first two essays here, were part of a collective effort to link formal analyses of film to political perspectives, and psychoanalysis was a crucial term in that conjunction. I have no desire to comment in detail on my own, much less others', work but the strengths and weaknesses of the psychoanalytic connection are clearer to me now than they were then.

If one is concerned to analyse art in its social and political context then one of the absolute necessities is to give an account of the processes of identification and disidentification, the methods by which fictions bind us into representations of both world and self. Psychoanalysis is the most developed theory of identification in the west, providing a whole array of concepts and procedures for following the mechanisms of identification. It is doubtful whether any serious contemporary analysis of social and cultural forms could ignore psychoanalytic method or insights. However, psychoanalysis finally comprehends all our complex identifications in terms of the fundamental identification of ourselves as sexed – as little boys or little girls. It is not simply that the problem with this theory of a fundamental identification is that it represents the difference between the sexes as the *necessary* basis for the recognition of further difference. One might argue against the position that there was any *necessity* in such a foundation while still admitting that sexual difference occupies a crucial place in our culture. What is really problematic is that psychoanalysis produces a theory of identity which does not allow for a genuine heterogeneity and contradiction in our diverse identifications. It does not simply make the claim that one difference is more important than all the others but articulates all further identifications in terms of a primary sexual identification.

It is now absolutely clear to me that it is on the basis of diverse and contradictory identifications that we must begin our accounts of politics and culture. It could be noticed, in passing, that the problems of diverse identifications surface within psychoanalysis in the heterogeneity of the neurotic, perverse and psychotic structures of identification co-existing within the individual. A sceptic might remark at this point that it is not identification which is being diversified but identity which is bleeding away in an unstoppable haemmorhage of difference. But the banality of endlessly finding the Many in place of the One is avoided by the concrete analysis of the processes of identification in particular fields of activity and struggle. Identity does not vanish but appears in relation to fields of practices and discourses often contradictory in both their internal and external relations. If the inevitable identities of race, class, age and sex impose (and that imposition insists daily), it is not because of some necessary features of biology or the forces of production but because of the practices and discourses which mobilise those biologies and those forces.

It is doubtful, given this perspective, whether one could produce a final theory of identity or identification; instead it will always be a question of using a variety of theories and scholarly methods in the investigation of particular unities of representation and practices, unities partly chosen in relation to divisions instituted by the academy, but, more importantly, in those vital obsessions where repetition may lead to liberating truths. In books as disparate as John Barrell's *The Dark Side of the Landscape*, Denise Riley's *War in the Nursery*, Jonathon Rosenbaum's *Moving Places*, Jacqueline Rose's *The Case of Peter Pan* and Edward Said's *Orientalism*, I glimpse a community of methods which takes us past the endless confrontation between the One and the Many, where the Master, in whatever mask, simply tells the same old story of fixed identity while the Legion of Difference promises the absolutely new and the absolutely different, right up to the gates of the university campus.

The acceptance of the diversity and the worldliness to which I am appealing also avoids the crippling weight of normative criticism which affects any fundamental theory of identification (Marxist or psychoanalytic) when it divides works of art in relation to criteria of identity which are automatically evaluative. In *Screen* the adopting of Lacanian forms of psychoanalytic argument had effectively reintroduced criteria of value which denigrated forms of popular cinema in favour of a certain number of politically avant-garde texts: Godard, Straub, Oshima etc. For those teachers who had looked to film theory to break out of the high art enclave, it had led firmly back there, albeit in a highly politicised version. As avant-garde positions were valorised, Hollywood was produced negatively: classic narrative Hollywood cinema was evaluated in terms of the constant placing of the spectator in a position of imaginary knowledge. This cinema was held to deprive the spectator of any perspective for social or political action except for privileged moments when vision was fleetingly disturbed by a pressure the text could not contain.

In my opinion it was this pattern of evaluation of the cinema which provided the most important area of disagreement when, in 1976, four of the board members most closely associated with secondary education chose both to resign from the magazine and to fight a campaign to gain control of the society. Unfortunately, however, the chosen battleground was psychoanalysis and in

11

their resignation statement the four criticised the magazine for adopting too uncritical an attitude to a psychoanalysis which was unproblematically identified with Lacan. Not only was Lacan's work held to be wilfully obscure but the use of its arcane vocabulary merely skated over the fact that analytic descriptions of the child's psychic formation were simply transposed to the adult spectator in the cinema despite the fact that the adult was characterised as having superseded the relations of the child. None of these criticisms were without their validity, and many were taken up in *Screen* over the next three years, but the debate polarised into an over simple battle between pro- and anti- psychoanalysis, pro- and anti- theory. Victory when it came was pyrrhic. The board lost its balance both in relation to those engaged in secondary education and those committed to Hollywood. If the years before 1977 had been for me a chance to participate in a carnival of ideas and education, the period after that was characterised by bitter enmity overlaid with blind ambition as *Screen*, in a major problem of its success, became important not just in terms of ideas and analysis but more materially as jobs appeared within various sectors, particularly tertiary education, in direct relation to the area of work laid out by *Screen*. As *Screen* got locked into bitter internal debate, much of the original energy and excitement of the original project was refound in the society's new magazine *Screen Education* where concerns both with secondary teaching and popular culture were very much to the fore.

On *Screen* itself there were serious efforts to take account of the discourses and institutions which, together with the narrative and visual economies of the film text, produce a variety of identifications and evaluations. But the status of psychoanalysis and, more importantly, Marxism were not sufficiently confronted. The magazine became for me not a pleasure or a liberation but a repressive duty. In 1978 I was one of those who proposed that the magazine transform itself so that it could address questions of the formation of popular taste in film and television. What was done was done slowly, half-heartedly and badly. By 1979 my engagement was minimal and in 1981 I finally came off the masthead. There was the possibility of a new era at *Screen* and it seemed churlish to remain as a monument to former enmities.

Many of the most bitter arguments after 1976 never reached the pages of the magazine but they focused on debates as to whether *Screen* should engage more directly with politics and with film-making practices, particularly the growing independent sector. With the benefit of hindsight, it is clear to me that both of these demands were absolutely correct in form and hopelessly wrong in content.

Throughout the seventies much work of cultural analysis on the left and particularly within *Screen* took place within a space articulated by the work of the French Marxist, Louis Althusser. Althusser, while stressing certain traditional Leninist themes, used elements from Mao Zedong and the French tradition in the philosophy of science, to propose forms of Marxist analysis which gave due weight to the spheres of politics and ideology. While Althusser held the economic to be the determining instance within society, both the political and the ideological instances had a 'relative autonomy' which entailed they had to be studied in their own specificity, and only in a much later moment related to the other instances. There was never any active engagement with Althusser's thought in the pages of *Screen* and his work was rarely quoted but he provided the intellectual space in which a specific analysis of a cultural form, in this case film and cinema, could be carried out in the conviction that, at a later date, this specificity could be related to the fundamental divisions of capital and labour and the ideological formations which played their part in the re-production of that division. This tenet of faith became increasingly difficult to uphold as, throughout the seventies, a series of texts were produced by people who had acted as editors of the Althusserian magazine *Theoretical Practice*. Tony Cutler, Barry Hindess, Paul Hirst and Athar Hussain both singly and together produced argument after argument to show the theoretical impasse of Althusser's position. Either the ideological and the political are autonomous from the economic and have their own effectivity, in which case any notion of defining the relations of production simply in economic terms becomes ridiculous, or they are not autonomous and then no matter how much 'complexity' is intro-duced into the analysis, economics will give you the 'real' relations of production and it will simply be a matter of specifying the 'modifications' of those relations introduced by their political or ideological representation, those representations themselves finally being determined in their operation by the 'real' economic relations. In other words, and more bluntly, we must decide whether classes are determined by relations of production which are understood to be given economically and independently of the political and ideological features of a social formation, *or* whether one can only theorise classes in terms of the oppositions and contradictions produced by the economic relations *and* their political and ideological representations.

It was in the context of this debate that I undertook my work on discourse and, in particular, on the work of the French philosopher and linguist Michel Pêcheux. If Althusserianism was genuinely to demonstrate the operations of ideology then it needed to analyse how a discourse functioned in the production of subjectivity and how class positions would alter that functioning. Pêcheux's work provided the most elaborate and detailed consideration of that problem and, for some two years, much of my intellectual work circled around his theses and formulations. The third essay in this collection, 'On discourse', bears witness to that time. The final conclusions of the piece are, however, negative. The commitment to the unity of bourgeois ideology, of an identity in terms of class which comes before any specific analyses, undercuts Pêcheux's many acute insights into the functioning of discourse and its subjective effects.

The essay is still written from a self-confidently Marxist position but its conclusions point away from any use of Marxist as a self-description except in terms either of intellectual formation or in terms of specific forms of analysis. If much Marxist theory of the relations between ideology and the economic base is unconvincing, if ideology itself becomes a paralysing concept insofar as it suggests a unified field of belief and subjectivity, Marx's actual analyses of that economic base still offer extremely important guides to a materialist analysis of culture. Marx's dissection of the labour process, of the working day or machinery and large-scale industry (chapters 7, 10, 15 or volume 1 of *Capital*) dissolve the 'evidence' provided by a factory or a political struggle in a complex play of heterogenous factors: laws, technical advances, economic determinants. It is in these specific analyses that Marx's continuing value would seem to reside and not in a theory of value which merely captured the central feature of early industrial production, nor in an account of ideology which retained the philosophic drive towards identity.

These considerations made notions of *Screen*'s engagement with politics extremely problematic. It was not a question of affiliating to already defined political struggles but of considering the conditions of the existence of political struggle, our own included. The effort was beyond us.

The call to engage with independent film was as contradictory. It was true that the independent sector had grown, it was true that many of the films made in the later seventies had been influenced by *Screen*, but it was also true that much of that influence had been catastrophic, linking a banal formalism to political didacticism in a formula which had nothing to recommend it – except to initiates.[2] To intervene in this situation *Screen* would have had to confront its inadequate engagement both with the image and with popular film. When *Screen*, in 1971, had been reconstituted it had eschewed the use of stills in its pages. Traditionally images were used within film magazines simply as illustrations and *Screen* was determined to investigate the functioning of the image rather than simply display it. In time *Screen* did develop a use of the image but it was in relation to very specific analyses of films. Such analyses were both illuminating and liberating, demonstrating the micro-levels at which the text articulated both itself and the spectator. The corresponding danger was that the image appeared to be exhausted by the analysis. The very practice of shot by shot analysis denied a certain specificity of the image, always reduced to its discursive representation. What *Screen* might seriously have considered were film-making projects but, as with the political task, the atmosphere of distrust and enmity was such that no positive collective action of any kind was possible.

Screen's political impasse was one generally shared on an academic left which had received its formation in the student movements of the late sixties and early seventies. For Althusser had not simply functioned as a theoretical master but as a political example. If one granted that the political and the ideological were autonomous and specific then it was quite possible to struggle within various institutions, particularly institutions of education, without necessarily taking up positions automatically designated as left by some outside political agency. The struggle was to fight for the progressive line within these institutions (and that progressive line might need to be elaborated) secure in the knowledge

15

that these struggles would finally come into convergence with the most fundamental economic and political struggles. Put crudely, Althusser enabled one to take institutions and ideas seriously while still genuinely retaining a belief in the reality of class struggle and revolution. In retrospect it is easy to mock the position as one of fundamental bad faith in which the strenuous aims of the revolution could always be left to other sectors while one battled away for small-scale reforms. Less cynically one might say that Althusser provided a way of taking seriously the reality of the institutions within which one worked without forgetting the reality of the desire to transform society. Seen from this political perspective, Althusser certainly takes his importance within the Eurocommunist movement of the seventies as western Communist parties tried to combine ever more serious commitment to the democratic institutions of capitalism together with a commitment to transform basic economic relations. Any European-wide chances for such a movement foundered in the autumn of 1977 when the French Communist Party broke the Union of the Left fearing that victory for that Union would find the Party's power reduced. As one who had lived in France, both just before and just after my undergraduate career, this reverse was indeed bitter. But the cup had to be drained to the dregs in the early part of 1979 when I took sabbatical leave in Paris. If work with Pêcheux was a constant delight, the intellectual and political atmosphere was poisonous. Many of the intellectuals who had profoundly influenced me as a student had effectively defected to the right, demonstrating how much of their leftism had simply been a response to Parisian fashions rather than any genuine commitment to the ideas and practices of '68. As one who had long railed against the insularity of English intellectuals, I was sickened by an intellectual community which either didn't realise, or couldn't afford to acknowledge, that much of what they were saying had been said better and with more honesty twenty-five years earlier by Camus.

At the same time China and Vietnam were proving again that nationalism (or, perhaps more frighteningly still, any ideology which offered fundamental forms of identification) was an infinitely more potent factor in political mobilisation than socialism, which can only ever offer the promises and possibilities of collective affiliation and combined effort. For me, much of the decade's previous political debate had been taken up with trying to marry the litanies of Leninism to the practices of Eurocommunism. Suddenly the whole vocabulary, so exciting a decade before, seemed barren. Krondstadt, the left turn in the Comintern, the transitional programme, the concept of the party, the struggle between revolution and reform – in France in 1979 the whole debate seemed merely antique. What I felt then, and have felt with increasing force ever since, is that all such talk was idle before the fact that the crisis facing socialism was nothing less than its re-invention – the necessity in the developed world of finding socialist goals and practices which would appeal to a very broad mass of the people. One lesson from Althusser remained: one must take the institutions seriously, struggle within them was crucial although it was no longer guaranteed, even at some vanishing point in the future, by a correct proletarian politics. But of struggle within the institution I was about to have my share.

Cambridge: the English Faculty
I have mentioned how, for me in 1973, the Cambridge English Faculty seemed a moribund and mediocre institution. Of course, there were individuals whose work compelled interest but they did not even begin to suggest either an intellectual or educational community. When I took up my Research Fellowship at Emmanuel College, Cambridge, I saw it as an opportunity to undertake individual research into literature, politics and language in the seventeenth century and to devote considerable time to work on film, which was not even formally recognised as a subject within the Faculty. By 1975, things had changed dramatically. The single most important factor was the arrival of Frank Kermode as King Edward VII Professor of English. Kermode is undoubtedly the outstanding English literary scholar and critic of his generation. By training a literary historian or philologist, much influenced by the Warburgian interest in the *Nachleben* (after life) of past works of art, he nevertheless was alive to much of the finest contemporary writing in both England and America, and most importantly, from my then rather limited viewpoint, he recognised clearly the importance both of Barthes and the intellectual revolution of the sixties in France. If he disagreed with much, it was a disagreement founded on a serious engagement with the

17

texts. At the same time as Kermode arrived, Raymond Williams was promoted to a professorial post, and a figure who had been tangential to the narrowly literary enterprise of much of Cambridge English acquried weight and authority. Although Williams could be described as a literary critic – he had written penetrating books on drama and the novel – he is more accurately characterised, in a self-invented category, as an analyst of culture and society. From the late fifties his books have sketched the relation between cultural forms and economic and political developments in genuinely original terms. Of a sudden Cambridge English looked a potentially serious endeavour as these professorial appointments provided a possible focus for a whole range of other teaching and research.

To understand the problems and possibilities in Cambridge in 1975, it is necessary to survey briefly the development of the English Faculty from the end of the first world war. Cambridge was late in producing an English Tripos, almost a century behind London and thirty years after Oxford. But this tardiness brought with it advantage. Elsewhere the subject had had to prove its scholarly credentials, stress philology and a grounding in Old and Middle English. At Cambridge in the aftermath of a war which had left even the most conservative institutions open to change, English could unashamedly aspire to be the centre of a new study of the humanities, a modern subject for modern times. It was in this propitious atmosphere that I. A. Richards went to see Mansfield Forbes, a keen mountaineer and the head of the new Tripos, to ask about the possibility of getting employment as a guide in the Highlands. The conversation turned to Coleridge and five hours later Richards was a lecturer in the new subject. Trained in philosophy by G. E. Moore and having returned to Cambridge to study medicine as a preliminary to taking up psychoanalysis, Richards was no narrow literary critic but a man committed to the study of communication of which he took literature to be *the* privileged instance. It was literature's ability to utilise fully the varied resources of language which enabled it to make available to the reader a complexity of experience which disappeared in other forms of communication. If Richards, in what is a constantly constitutive moment of English as a subject, saw compulsory education and mass circulation newspapers as promoting literacy but degrading literature, his pedagogic enterprise was admirably democratic. Every citizen must be enabled to participate in the reading of great literature and thus to increase their possibilities of experience. This is the project of Richards's teaching in the twenties: to devise methods of close reading, practical criticism, which will enable the individual reader to escape the prejudices ingrained by a degraded education and confront the literary text in all its complexity.

If it was Richards who developed the methods of Cambridge English in the twenties, it was Leavis who used those methods at the service of a complex ideology of literature in the thirties. Richards's presuppositions were democratic and ahistorical: everyone must be brought into unmediated contact with the unchanging psychological artefacts that are great literature; Leavis's were elitist and historical: the reading of the poem was not grounded in a set of psychological reactions shared by all but was a collective effort of argument and assent. Such collective activity was limited to that minority who could intelligently contribute to such discussion. And the task was vital. Since the seventeenth century, human relations had been progressively destroyed by a society which had divorced thought from feeling and the pace had quickened immeasurably with the onset of industrialism and utilitarianism. Marxism, far from being an alternative to capitalism, was simply its mirror-image. The crucial social and political effort was to recover the possibilities guaranteed by the living language of great literature and thus to rehumanise the world. Stated thus baldly seems not only futile but deeply silly. So to regard it ignores the extent to which, especially in the thirties, it served to articulate an opposition to capitalism without lapsing into the kind of economistic Marxism that Leavis demolished so thoroughly in 'Under which King, Bezonian?', an article which he published in *Scrutiny* at the end of the decade. It is also to ignore the generations of devoted schoolteachers who saw in Leavis's formulations a justification of their lives which did not reduce them to producers of office-fodder. But perhaps the most important element missing from my brief caricature of Leavis's position is the immense con-temporary force of the writings of Lawrence and Eliot which gave much vital sense to the Leavisite position of the thirties.

By the sixties, however, the thing was dead. The educational narrowness of the audience, the strident enunciation of the same

19

restricted canon, the increasingly ritual gestures of honesty and affront combined to induce paralysis. The reference to the close analysis of language had been replaced by the repetition of agreed readings, the engagement with modernism had frozen literary development at Lawrence. It was in this context that two challenges were mounted to the Leavisite account of literature and language (and whatever the posture of exclusion, the Leavisite account was, by and large, the Cambridge account).

Internally, there was the challenge posed by Raymond Williams. A Cambridge graduate, he returned to teach in the Faculty in 1961. Much of the force of Leavis's work in the thirties had been his insistence on the poet as a member of a wider linguistic community, drawing on resources of language which were both social and personal. This emphasis on what one might term the sociality of language was increasingly abandoned as the focus became the ever-more isolated author producing living language when all around was dead. Williams's attention to language was close, but it was never simply to the individual text but to the discourses and arguments in which the text found its meaning. *Culture and Society* investigated the shifting meaning of these two crucial terms as they were differently articulated through the nineteenth and twentieth centuries. Williams was developing a real study of the sociality of language and, together with this study, went a very different attitude to cultural developments. It was not the steady decline from an idealised organic community that interested Williams, but the long revolution in which ever greater sections of the population found a voice and a possibility of speaking. These possibilities might not only be found in the changing forms of high culture, themselves always, amongst other things, forms of exclusion, but in the academically despised popular forms of music hall, film and television.

If Williams offered one possibility for a serious renewal in the study of language and literature, another was offered by George Steiner. Steiner came as a Fellow to Churchill College in the early sixties and was, shamefully, never appointed to a lectureship. However, College Fellows did give occasional courses of lectures and Steiner's were not only brilliantly delivered and massively attended but also expounded new methods and conceptions in the study of language and literature. On the one hand there were the immensely powerful tools of structural analysis developed

20

by Jakobson and Lévi-Strauss, but even more important was the kind of radical semiotics practised by Barthes which, drawing on sources as diverse as Saussure and Nietzsche, argued for the primacy of language over the subject; which read the author not as the conscious controller but as the unconscious effect of the systems of language that went to make up the text. If Steiner himself always remained sceptical about this more radical version, his lectures made available to a wide audience in Cambridge continental work which offered an approach to literature and language which differed both from the exhausted tradition of practical criticism or Williams's energetic project to locate literary and linguistic forms in relation to patterns of economic and political domination.

In 1969 when I joined the English Faculty to read for Part 2 of the Tripos, I had already spent two years studying philosophy at Cambridge. The philosophy course was narrow but rigorous, little history of philosophy and nothing outside the Anglo-Saxon analytic tradition, but a thorough grounding in logic and the philosophy of science and, most important of all, a saturation in Wittgenstein and Quine. After the coherence of the philosophy course, the English Tripos seemed a total shambles. The conception of language at work was a debased form of Leavis and Richards, indeed the founding texts of Richards seemed totally forgotten, or certainly unread. It wasn't simply that there was no knowledge of structuralism, of Barthes's re-reading of the literary tradition or Heidegger's meditation on poetry. There wasn't even any awareness of the way in which Wittgenstein or Austin demanded a reconsideration of the relations between literature and language. As a final straw, modern literature seemed to begin and end with Lawrence and Eliot. Little Joyce or Pound, less Larkin and O'Hara, and no Moorcock or Ballard, Film, television and rock music simply didn't exist.

Amongst the exceptions to this rule of ignorant banality, the striking example was a very young lecturer called Stephen Heath. I shall never forget the excitement of his lecture course on realism in the European novel. Each week one climbed aboard a roller-coaster of ideas which deposited one stomachless two hours later, wondering if one had the courage to return for more. If late Wittgenstein stressed the way in which both world and speaker only appeared within a set of practices and discourses, what he terms a 'language game', he offered only a static picture of such games, which gave no indication of contradiction and change, of class or sexuality. It was these emphases that Heath brought to his treatment of the European novel. Realism was located as a particular historical practice, a method of writing which placed both reader and world outside any activity of signification. The modernism of Proust, Joyce and Mann was to disrupt this neutral practice, drawing attention to the text's construction of both reader and world and the sexual and political identities bound into those constructions. The novel as language game, but under the aspect of time and change, ravaged by death and sexuality.

The choice of Joyce's language as my topic of research when I graduated in 1971 was partly determined by those lectures and partly by my own background. To a first generation Irish immigrant, educated by monks, Joyce's texts spoke of very specific liberations. If Barthes's and Derrida's radical semiotics provided much of the vocabulary and method to analyse Joyce's use of language and narrative, these uses had still to be related to Ireland at the turn of the century. No aspect of Ireland's situation was more crucial for Joyce than the fact that English language and English literature were both inheritance and oppression. And that paradox is not limited to Ireland in 1900 on the verge of national liberation. It reverberates down the twentieth century both within England while a class, defined by Johnson as speechless, begins to find a voice, and throughout the world as the British empire gives way to the empire of English. It was this perspective that produced my second reservation about the *Tel Quel* position that had been developed at the end of the sixties. If, on the one hand, the valorisation of certain forms of modernist writing ignored almost all popular forms of culture and most traditional socialist politics (and it was these problems that *Screen* had helped me to focus) it also underestimated the complexity of the literary tradition and, most importantly, its relation to language and education. Barthes's characterisation of the break between the classic and the modern was of vital importance, for modernism was the product of a radically new positioning of the literary text in relation to both audience and sexuality. However it was also, as Kermode had convincingly indicated in the final chapter of *The Classic*, hopelessly reductive. Barthes collapsed all pre-modern writing into an unacceptable homogeneity which took no account of the histories of language, education or genre. I felt increasingly that the very abstract references to Saussure (or, less frequently and more elliptically, to Chomsky) were not adequate to the task proposed. In particular I wanted to find terms for describing the relations between language, literature and politics in the period 1580–1660 when both the English language and English literature took on recognisably modern forms. Joyce's determination to finish with English literature had, at one level, been singularly unsuccessful. I was now obsessed by going back to its beginnings to understand the persistence of the beast.

When, therefore, in February 1976, the Faculty advertised a post in English language since 1500 in relation to literature, they advertised the job that I most wanted to undertake in the academic world. My only hesitation about applying was that I didn't yet possess some of the necessary competences. If I was very familiar with theories of literary language, I had no professional competence either in the detailed analyses of contemporary linguistics or in the history of modern and early modern English. The Appointments Committee was obviously convinced by my undisguised zeal to master these fields and I was appointed from October 1976.

The next two and a half years were a period in which I worked so hard that, even now, I feel physically ill when I think of it. I had to train myself in a wide variety of linguistics and familiarise myself with the history of the language since 1500 while constructing and teaching courses for which there were no existing models. However, the linguistics department and John Bromwich, the senior philologist in the English Faculty, were both kind and helpful, and by the time I took a sabbatical in France at the beginning of 1979 I felt that I had justified the Appointment Committee's confidence and was happy to teach across a range of language and literature.

More intellectually important, I had obtained answers to many of the questions that had obsessed me in 1976, although the answers were largely negative. The dream of the automatic analysis of discourse (the title of Pêcheux's first book)[3] had given way to a recognition that the constitution of the corpus and the finding of regularities within it could not be divorced from the analyst's desire. Milton could not be submitted to a set of automatic operations which would provide the fundamental equivalences from which his text took meaning. So vast and various was the possible range of linguistic regularities that those identified would always depend on the initial approach to the text. And just as the text took its form in a dizzyingly vast series of determinations, so did the reader approaching it. This problem did not preclude analysis, it simply entailed that the analysis would depend on the reader as well as the text. Furthermore, if the spectre of endless difference could not be dispelled theoretically (for every reader a different meaning, for every reading a different meaning), in practice certain questions around sexuality and power, education and the national language impose shared approaches. The texts come to us in our time and respond to our (sometimes new) questions. Those questions must find their validity across a range of shared practices, including the professionally academic. Furthermore, the text's responses must always be couched in the accents of the past, no reading can ignore the range of historical possibilities of meaning. Exactly how to determine the range of historical possibility, how to respect the difference of the past without freezing it into an identity are theoretical problems that remain. What the concluding footnotes to the 'On discourse' paper and the whole of the essay 'Language, linguistics and the study of literature' demonstrate is that while linguistic description will be crucial and linguistic theory helpful in our reading of literary texts, there can be no question of a theory that will produce the meanings of literary texts. Those meanings are produced in response to specific practices of analysis.

Such analyses will need to take account of how language functions as the field and condition of desire. This functioning, however, is not atemporal but is dispersed across the material distribution of language, a distribution determined by technology and education, constrained by economics and genre. It is these questions which are addressed in the final paper of this collection: 'Realism: Balzac and Barthes', and that paper resolves, at least to my temporary satisfaction, the tension between the two opposing conceptions of language which had obsessed me for more than a decade: language as power and language as desire, language in and out of time.[4]

The final paper, however, also contains some brief reflections partially prompted by my experience of leaving Cambridge. The advertisement of the post of language and literature in 1976 was not designed to fit my particular intellectual interests but was part of a confused attempt to find new bases for the teaching of English. To understand that attempt and its failure, we must return to 1969 and the shambles which I had first experienced as a student. That experience was not a merely personal one for the structure of the English degree was crumbling under a variety of pressures. A curriculum which had survived unchallenged for forty years, even at the height of the Leavisite controversies, was increasingly seen as irrelevant.

The English degree at Cambridge is divided into two parts: the first two years are a traditional survey course of English literature, life and thought from Chaucer to the present day; the final year is a more specialist affair where together with some compulsory papers, of which Tragedy is the most important, the student could choose to study particular authors or periods. By 1969, the whole structure was coming under fire. Students, inspired by the example of '68, wanted more opportunity to determine their own study, more access to the brave new thoughts which seemed to circulate everywhere but in the teaching of the Faculty. Throughout the early seventies, the Faculty reacted by making the Part Two more and more flexible, particularly through the introduction of dissertations to replace some exams. Part Two became a licence for a student to write his or her own course of study and in this atmosphere of flexibility much good and interesting work was done.

Part One, however, remained more or less totally unchanged and it was here that the real educational and ideological problems resided. If, in the thirties, it was accepted that a student could read through the literature of 600 years, this was because on the one hand there was more or less complete agreement on the relatively small quantity of material which made up that literature, and one could reasonably expect that the student would be familiar with that material even before he or she arrived at university. Neither of these conditions now applied. As literary criticism had institutionalised itself throughout the twentieth century, it had multiplied its subject matter. More and more authors could be deemed worthy of study and the most established ones grew in volume. Where once you could read *Paradise Lost* and Keats's *Odes*, now you had to read Cowley, Crashaw and the whole of Milton, Leigh Hunt, Thomas Love Peacock and the whole of the major Romantics. If that wasn't already a ludicrous task, the secondary literature had proliferated: not just literary criticism but social history, anthropology and a host of other disciplines which could bring their relevance to bear. And this mammoth task faced students who were less and less equipped to undertake it, who lacked many competences earlier taken for granted: knowledge of classical literature, knowledge of the Christian religion and the Authorised Version, knowledge of grammar.

An argument was developing, articulated most ably by Stephen Heath at Faculty meeting after Faculty meeting, that the Part One should be reduced to a year in which the student would be trained in certain skills of reading and analysis before going on to a Part Two which would allow a student to opt between a conventional literary course and a more wide ranging series of cultural studies. With Kermode's arrival and Williams moving from the margin to the centre of the Faculty, much seemed possible. When in the Lent term of 1976, the entire Faculty narrowly voted against a consideration of reform of the Tripos a group, which included many of the active teaching officers in the Faculty, determined to set up an informal Tripos reform group under the chairmanship of Kermode. My appointment came just before this group convened and I fondly imagined that I would soon be playing a part in a revived and exciting Cambridge degree. Disillusion came quickly. The committee chaired by Kermode could not bring itself to adopt the truly radical Part One that had been proposed by Stephen Heath. Although some favoured it, others could not give up the idea that coverage was essential to an English degree. The result was a series of compromises which were decisively rejected. The chance, if indeed there had ever been one, had come and gone.

However, I still had my own job to get on with, although I was quickly made to recognise how difficult that task was going to be. On my appointment I had been asked not only to undertake my own teaching but to organise and coordinate language teaching in the Faculty. Invited at the beginning of 1977 to present my proposals to the Faculty Board, I had no sooner been welcomed by the chairman than my presence was challenged by a professor and I was required to leave the meeting. My proposals were never discussed; instead the basis of my appointment was questioned and I found myself deprived of any responsibility for organisation and co-ordination. I had realised that my appointment had been controversial, one member of the Appointments Committee had resigned over it, but I had no conception of how deep the enmity could run. The next month I was invited on to the committee in charge of postgraduate affairs. Another professor resigned and only resumed his place when, advised by sympathetic elders, I declined to take up my invitation.

This degree of institutional hostility to a young lecturer in his first year of teaching is still something that I find both shocking and shameful. If the aim was to demoralise me, however, I was exceptionally fortunate in the support I could receive in my college. On my appointment to a university post I had moved to a fellowship in King's and into an atmosphere of intellectual co-operation and comradeship which I doubt that I will be lucky enough to know again. If Emmanuel had been kind to me, King's allowed the possibility of a really joyful learning. I took up my Fellowship with David Simpson and Norman Bryson and every meeting on student business became an intellectual education. As immediate mentors we had John Barrell and Tony Tanner, who returned from the States in 1977, and it was always possible to ask advice from Frank Kermode or Dadie Rylands. If it was clear that there was no real chance of change in the Faculty, King's offered a world of intellectual excitement in which to both work and teach. And this we did. Books and articles were produced in profusion, large numbers of students left with a real grounding in the reading of literature and good degrees. That was the rub. Finally, the Faculty could not be ignored and it was the annual purgatory of exams which reminded one of this forcibly. If our candidates continued to do well, it was in the context of continual attempts to impose a very narrow version of a literary curriculum in both the setting and the marking of exams.

I was also denied research students. When I first took up my lectureship, I was assigned a couple of research students and another one the next year but after that, despite the success of my first pupils, I was sent no more. It became clear to me in time that students who asked to be supervised by me were dissuaded from such a rash course of action and that, in one particular case, a supervisor had been sought outside the university rather than have a pupil allocated to me. Finally a particularly egregious case came to my attention and I demanded an explanation from the Degree Secretary. This man, whom I had always admired, told me, in what I can only describe as an embarrassed manner, that he was merely the servant of a committee some of whose members thought that 'I influenced my students too much'. Under the impact of this Socratic compliment, I determined to leave Cambridge once I had been upgraded.

Upgrading is a procedure peculiar to Cambridge which is the only British university to retain the post of assistant lecturer. These are non-renewable five year appointments but when they come to an end the Faculty Board has the option of recommending the creation of a new permanent lectureship to which the assistant lecturer is then appointed. It is this process that is known as upgrading. I had assumed that the original opposition to my appointment had been based on the understandable grounds that I did not possess all the competences that the job required. The original Appointments Committee, faced with a field in which no single candidate had all the competences they had hoped for, had backed me as the candidate most likely to acquire the skills that I did not already possess. This I had done and when I introduced a new form of the History of the Language paper into Part Two of the Tripos, I thought that I had accomplished all that I had been asked to do. Given this, and my publication and teaching record, I felt that my upgrading would be quasi-automatic. I was rudely disillusioned. The Faculty Board when it met to discuss my case debated for hours before reaching an inconclusive vote. At a second and extra-ordinary meeting of the Board and after more lengthy and bitter discussion, the Board decided by one vote (10–9) to create a lectureship to which I be appointed. The depth of fear and loathing which had been revealed in this process astonished me, not least because discussion seemed largely to have turned around my work on Joyce, the original reason that I had been appointed. However, as I had, perhaps foolishly, never doubted a successful outcome and as I knew of no one whom I respected in the least who had voted against me, the summer proved quite bearable.

Winter was different. There was still a further administrative formality in that an Appointments Committee had to appoint me to the newly created post. In October 1980, at the start of my fifth year lecturing in Cambridge, that Committee voted against me by four votes to three in a move unprecedented in the history of the English Faculty. It was only at this point that the astonishing levels of envy, hatred and animosity that I aroused began to depress me. Early on in my appointment, as people seemed to resign at the mention of my name, I had talked to I. A. Richards, back in Cambridge in retirement, about how to deal with such petty institutional animosities. His advice was to keep working: both as a means of retaining one's own sanity and as the most appropriate response to local jealousies. In the Michaelmas term of 1980, for the first time, I found this advice difficult to follow. But if there was bitterness and envy verging on hatred within the English Faculty, I was heartened by the degree of friendship and affection I found in the university. Most important was the constant support from my contemporaries at King's and the unyielding friendship of Stephen Heath. In addition, throughout the university, and particularly in my old colleges of Emmanuel and Trinity, I was astonished and pleased by the expressions of support I received. The university authorities, particularly the Vice-Chancellor, Sir Peter Swinnerton-Dyer were as helpful as they could be, but Cambridge University's devolved structure leaves Appointments Committees sovereign, and, short of suspending the Faculty, there was little the university could do. Nevertheless, at the end of the Michaelmas term the Appointments Committee reconsidered my case. This time the vote was four to three in my favour, but five votes are needed to secure an appointment and I was out. King's, where the Provost Bernard Williams had been infinitely supportive, offered to keep me on as a College Lecturer but I had no desire to remain in Cambridge without a Faculty job. Before the first Appointments Committee had met in October and when I thought my future secure, I had been applying for jobs elsewhere. In April 1981 I was appointed to a professorship of English at Strathclyde University.

In between these two events, the country had been treated to the amazing spectacle of the 'structuralist controversy'. By calling a debate in the University Senate, my supporters brought the case into the public arena and the newspapers had a field day. Fortunately I was on sabbatical throughout the term or my always incipient megalomania would have turned terminal. By calling me a structuralist my opponents revealed their ignorance about both structuralism and my own work. If, however, they had admitted the real terms of the debate – under what terms and with what methods could you continue to teach English language and literature – then they would have already conceded what they were desperate to defend: that there could be no questions about English as a discipline. For them, English had no history. It had been, was, and would continue to be. What was strange was that, unlike the mid-seventies, there was no chance that the basic curriculum and assumptions of Cambridge English could be challenged. In retrospect I can only suppose that the bitterness was engendered by the fact that if the traditionalists had won the votes they had lost all the arguments. My reappointment made me perhaps the most visible example of that intellectual challenge. Not content with sacking me, however, the Faculty, in the same term, voted both Kermode and Williams, its most eminent members, off the appointments committee, a root to branch solution to all future intellectual problems.

It might be expected that the events at Cambridge might have further embittered me against academic institutions, convinced me of the need for a political cleansing of the Augean academic stables. In fact, the effects were very different. It was quite clear to me that the debate at Cambridge could not be reduced to a political difference. If the arguments about the teaching of English had political effects – in terms of our relation to our past literary culture, in terms of the teaching of English language and literature in both school and university – those effects could not be mapped on to an already existing political argument. What became evident to me in the course of the fight at Cambridge simply confirmed what my experiences on *Screen* had already suggested: there could be no comfortable divisions between politics and the humanities. Both the humanities and the social sciences are always both inside and outside the campus, always reacting to social and cultural developments but always within disciplines whose authority can never be simply or lightly dismissed. I suggest something of that argument in the final paper, its fuller elaboration would need to consider education in all its aspects.

The final paper also sketches an argument about the current institutionalisation of 'theory' within English studies. To address that problem fully would require not just another essay but another book. It cannot, however, be stressed too often that theory only and ever makes sense in relation to practice. The practices to which literary theory must always address itself are those that regulate our relation to a literary tradition which is both inheritance and oppression. The two crucial practices here are education, and that involves questions from the provisions of doctoral programmes to the first steps in reading and writing, and contemporary culture, not just the novelist, poets, dramatists whose relation to the literary tradition is relatively clear but also television and the cinema which have displaced the book so radically in our times.[5] Any theories which ignore those practices are just so much tired mumblings of superiority, so many smug attempts to evade the pressing and important questions about our past and its present.

But these questions bring me to the limit of this collection and into the present at Strathclyde where the experience of teaching new graduate courses and the opportunity of new contact with the secondary schools have answered some questions and posed many more. This collection relates largely to questions and answers developed at Cambridge or on *Screen* and I want to limit this reflection to that time. As I travelled on the train to London in the summer of 1981, as in the archaic language of Cambridge I 'came down' for the last time, I was conscious of both sadness and expectancy. Sadness at leaving those friends with whom conversation was always dialogue, exchange always dialectic. Sadness too at the chance that had been missed in the mid-seventies to redefine the aims and methods of a 'literary education'. But also expectancy. When I was first accepted as a student at Cambridge it had been to read history. Since then I had traversed the disciplines of philosophy, English, film and linguistics. If I was now a well-qualified jack of all trades, it was time to put some of those skills to work in the practical business of constructing courses that would educate and liberate. That work continues.

Theoretical essays

Notes

1. Roland Barthes, *Essais critiques* (Le Seuil, Paris, 1971), p. 13.
2. It would be wrong to think that *Screen* was the only influence in this process – the history of independent film in the seventies has yet to be written. It would also be wrong to condemn out of hand all those films which were formally experimental and politically concerned – Phil Mulloy's *In the Forest* or Laura Mulvey and Peter Wollen's *Penthesilea* are only two examples of films that created and used new spaces in the cinema. Nevertheless, much that was produced then did conform to an over-theoretical formula, which did little to stimulate a real political and formal engagement with the cinema.
3. The title of Pêcheux's first book was *L'Analyse automatique du discours* (Dunod, Paris, 1969). The correct translation into English would be 'Computer analysis of discourse'. But in the ambiguity of the French 'automatique', I, at least, find a trace of the perverse utopian dream, which I shared, to discover an 'automatic' method of processing texts which would reveal their fundamental equivalences independently of the desire of any analyst.
4. I have retained the form in which the paper was delivered at the conference because of the importance of that conference in clarifying my ideas.
5. I have left out of account here the whole question of the relation of TV and film to literature courses. This is a vexed question and in the present context I will suffice myself with two brief points. First, I am convinced that TV and Film should be taught within English courses. Second I am convinced that much of the hostility I encountered was because of my work in television and film although it comprised only a tiny part of my teaching – two very short courses in five years.

Realism and the cinema: notes on some Brechtian theses

Throughout his life Brecht conducted, together with a continually experimenting artistic practice, a sustained theoretical reflection on his own and others' work. In the early thirties drawing up a project for a new critical review Brecht wrote

> Amongst other things the review understands the word 'criticism' in its double sense – transforming *dialectically* the totality of subjects into a *permanent crisis* and thus conceiving the epoch as a critical period in both meanings of the term. And this point of view necessarily entails a rehabilitation of theory in its productive rights.
>
> (XVIII, 85 – 6)[1]

The importance of theory and its productive effects in the aesthetic domain persists as a central concern throughout Brecht's writings. Two areas in which Brecht felt the need for theory to be particularly pressing were the debate on realism in which Lukács's positions achieved dominance in the early thirties and the relatively new cultural area of the cinema. His reflections on these topics were published in 1967 under the titles *Über den Realismus* and *Über Film* and these sections have since been totally translated into French and sections of them have recently been published in English.[2] The aim of this article is to elaborate some of the positions advanced in those two works. It is not an attempt to extract a coherent theory from Brecht's theoretical writings (and still less to offer a coherent account of the relation of this theory to his artistic practice) but rather a set of digressions which take as their starting point some Brechtian theses.

Theoretical essays

The classic realist text

> Criticism, at least Marxist criticism, must proceed methodically and concretely in each case, in short scientifically. Loose talk is of no help here, whatever its vocabulary. In no circumstances can the necessary guide-lines for a practical definition of realism be derived from literary works alone. (Be like Tolstoy – but without his weaknesses! Be like Balzac – only up-to-date!) Realism is an issue not only for literature: it is a major political, philosophical and practical issue and must be handled and explained as such – as a matter of general human interest.
>
> (XIX, 307)[3]

One of the difficulties of any discussion about realism is the lack of any really effective vocabulary with which to discuss the topic. Most discussions turn on the problems of the production of discourse which will fully adequate the real. This notion of adequacy is accepted both by the realists and indeed by the anti-realists whose main argument is that no discourse can ever be adequate to the multifarious nature of the real. This notion of the real is, however, I wish to suggest, a notion which is tied to a particular type of literary production – the nineteenth-century realist novel. The dominance of this novel form is such that people still tend to confuse the general question of realism with the particular forms of the nineteenth-century realist novel. In order to make the discussion clearer I want therefore to attempt to define the structure which typifies the nineteenth-century realist novel and to show how that structure can also be used to describe a great number of films. The detour through literature is necessary because, in many ways, the structure is much more obvious there and also because of the historical dominance of the classic realist novel over much film production. What to a large extent will be lacking in this article is the specific nature of the film form but this does not seem to me to invalidate the setting up of certain essential categories from which further discussion must progress. The structure I will attempt to disengage I shall call the classic realist text and I shall apply it to novels and films.

A classic realist text may be defined as one in which there is a hierarchy amongst the discourses which compose the text and this hierarchy is defined in terms of an empirical notion of truth. Perhaps the easiest way to understand this is through a reflection on the use of inverted commas within the classic realist novel. While those sections in the text which are contained in inverted commas may cause a certain difficulty for the reader – a certain confusion vis-à-vis what really is the case – this difficulty is abolished by the unspoken (or more accurately the unwritten) prose that surrounds them. In the classical realist novel the narrative prose functions as a metalanguage that can state all the truths in the object language – those words held in inverted commas – and can also explain the relation of this object language to the real. The metalanguage can thereby explain the relation of this object language to the world and the strange methods by which the object languages attempt to express truths which are straightforwardly conveyed in the metalanguage. What I have called an unwritten prose (or a metalanguage) is exactly that language, which while placing other languages between inverted commas and regarding them as certain material expressions which express certain meanings, regards those same meanings as finding transparent expression within the metalanguage itself. Transparent in the sense that the metalanguage is not regarded as material; it is dematerialised to achieve perfect representation – to let the identity of things shine through the window of words. For in so far as the metalanguage is treated itself as material – it, too, can be reinterpreted; new meanings can be found for it in a further metalanguage. The problem is the problem that has troubled western thought since the pre-Socratics recognised the separation between what was said and the act of saying. This separation must be thought both as time and space – as the space, which in the distance from page to eye or mouth to ear allows the possibility of misunderstanding – as the time taken to traverse the page or listen to an utterance which ensures the deferred interpretation of words which are always only defined by what follows. The problem is that in the moment that we say a sentence the meaning (what is said) seems fixed and evident but what is said does not exist solely for the moment and is open to further interpretations. Even in this formulation of the problem I have presupposed an original moment when there is strict contemporaneity between the saying and what is said, but the difficulty is more radical for there is no such original moment. The separation is always already there as we cannot locate the presence of what is said – distributed as it is through space – nor the present of what is said – distributed as it is through time.

This separation bears witness to the real as articulated. The thing represented does not appear in a moment of pure identity as it tears itself out of the world and presents itself, but rather is caught in an articulation in which each object is defined in a set of differences and oppositions.

It is this separation that the unwritten text attempts to *anneal*, to make whole, through denying its own status as writing – as marks of material difference distributed through time and space. Whereas other discourses within the text are considered as material which are open to re-interpretation, the narrative discourse simply allows reality to appear and denies its own status as articulation. This relationship between discourses can be clearly seen in the work of such a writer as George Eliot. In the scene in *Middlemarch* where Mr Brooke goes to visit the Dagleys' farm we read two different languages. One is the educated, well-meaning, but not very intelligent discourse of Mr Brooke and the other is the uneducated, violent and very nearly unintelligible discourse of the drunken Dagley. But the whole dialogue is surrounded by a metalanguage, which being unspoken is also unwritten, and which places these discourses in inverted commas and can thus discuss these discourses' relation to truth – a truth which is illuminatingly revealed in the metalanguage. The metalangauge reduces the object languages into a simple division between form and content and extracts the meaningful content from the useless form. One can see this process at work in the following passage which ends the scene:

> He [Mr Brooke] had never been insulted on his own land before, and had been inclined to regard himself as a general favourite (we are all apt to do so, when we think of our own amiability more than what other people are likely to want of us). When he had quarrelled with Caleb Garth twelve years before he had thought that the tenants would be pleased at the landlord's taking everything into his own hands.
>
> Some who follow the narrative of this experience may wonder at the midnight darkness of Mr Dagley; but nothing was easier in those times than for a hereditary farmer of his grade to be ignorant, in spite somehow of having a rector in the twin parish who was a gentleman to the backbone, a curate nearer at hand who preached more learnedly than the rector, a landlord who had gone into everything, especially fine art and social improvement and all the lights of Middlemarch only three miles off.　　　　　　　　　　　(Eliot 1967:432–3)

This passage provides the necessary interpretations for the discourses that we have read earlier in the chapter. Both the discourses of Dagley and Mr Brooke are revealed as springing from two types of ignorance which the metalanguage can expose and reveal. So we have Mr Brooke's attitude to what his tenants thought of him contrasted with the reality which is available through the narrative prose. No discourse is allowed to speak for itself but rather it must be placed in a context which will reduce it to a simple explicable content. And in the claim that the narrative prose has direct access to a final reality we can find the claim of the classic realist novel to present us with the truths of human nature. The ability to reveal the truth about Mr Brooke is the ability that guarantees the generalisations of human nature.

Thus then a first definition of the classic realist text – but does this definition carry over into films where it is certainly less evident where to locate the dominant discourse? It seems to me that it does and in the following fashion. The narrative prose achieves its position of dominance because it is in the position of knowledge and this function of knowledge is taken up in the cinema by the narration of events. Through the knowledge we gain from the narrative we can split the discourses of the various characters from their situation and compare what is said in these discourses with what has been revealed to us through narration. The camera shows us what happens – it tells the truth against which we can measure the discourses. A good example of this classical realist structure is to be found in Pakula's film *Klute*. This film is of particular interest because it was widely praised for its realism on its release. Perhaps even more significantly it tended to be praised for its realistic presentation of the leading woman, Bree (played by Jane Fonda).

In *Klute* the relationship of dominance between discourses is peculiarly accentuated by the fact that the film is interspersed with fragments of Bree talking to her psychiatrist. This subjective discourse can be exactly measured against the reality provided by the unfolding of the story. Thus all her talk of independence is portrayed as finally an illusion as we discover, to no great surprise but to our immense relief, what she really wants is to settle down in the mid-West with John Klute (the detective played by Donald Sutherland) and have a family. The final sequence of the film is particularly telling in this respect. While

Klute and Bree pack their bags to leave, the soundtrack records Bree at her last meeting with her psychiatrist. Her own estimation of the situation is that it most probably won't work but the reality of the image ensures us that this is the way it will really be. Indeed Bree's monologue is even more interesting – for in relation to the reality of the image it marks a definite advance on her previous statements. She has gained insight through the plot development and like many good heroines of classic realist texts her discourse is more nearly adequate to the truth at the end of the film than at the beginning. But if a progression towards knowledge is what marks Bree, it is possession of knowledge which marks the narrative, the reader of the film and John Klute himself. For Klute is privileged by the narrative as the one character whose discourse is also a discourse of knowledge. Not only is Klute a detective and thus can solve the problem of his friend's disappearance – he is also a man, and a man who because he has not come into contact with the city has not had his virility undermined. And it is as a full-blooded man that he can know not only the truth of the mystery of the murders but also the truth of the woman Bree. Far from being a film which goes any way to portraying a woman liberated from male definition (a common critical response), *Klute* exactly guarantees that the real essence of woman can only be discovered and defined by a man.

The analysis sketched here is obviously very schematic but what, hopefully, it does show is that the structure of the classic realist text can be found in film as well. That narrative of events – the knowledge which the film provides of how things really are – is the metalanguage in which we can talk of the various characters in the film. What would still remain to be done in the elaboration of the structure of the classic realist text in cinema is a more detailed account of the actual mechanisms by which the narrative is privileged (and the way in which one or more of the characters within the narrative can be equally privileged) and also a history of the development of this dominant narrative. On the synchronic level it would be necessary to attempt an analysis of the relationship between the various types of shot and their combination into sequences – are there for example certain types of shot which are coded as subjective and therefore subordinate to others which are guaranteed as objective? In addition how does music work as the guarantee or otherwise of truth? On the dia-chronic level it would be necessary to study how this form was produced – what relationship obtains between the classic realist text and technical advances such as the development of the talkie? What ideological factors were at work in the production and dominance of the classic realist text?

To return, however, to the narrative discourse. It is necessary to attempt to understand the type of relations that this dominant discourse produces. The narrative discourse cannot be mistaken in its identifications because the narrative discourse is not present as discourse – as articulation. The unquestioned nature of the narrative discourse entails that the only problem that reality poses is to go and look and see what *Things* there are. The relationship between the reading subject and the real is placed as one of pure specularity. The real is not articulated – it is. These features imply two essential features of the classic realist text:

1 The classic realist text cannot deal with the real as contra-dictory.
2 In a reciprocal movement the classic realist text ensures the position of the subject in a relation of dominant specularity.

The classic realist text as progressive art

> In general, do not be content with providing an insight into the literature of the country in question, but follow the details of literary life itself. Consider literary phenomena as events and as social events. (Principles for the review *Das Wort*) (XIX, 307)[4]

It may be objected that the account that I have given of the classic literary text is deficient in the following extremely important fashion. It ignores what is the usual criterion for realism, that is to say subject matter. The category of the classic realist text lumps together in book and film *The Grapes of Wrath* and *The Sound of Music*, *L'Assommoir* and *Toad of Toad Hall*. In order to find a criterion with which to make distinctions within the area of the classic realist text it is necessary to reflect on contra-diction. I have stated that the classic realist text cannot deal with the real in its contradiction because of the unquestioned status of the representation at the level of the dominant discourse. In order to understand how contradiction can be dealt with it is necessary to investigate the workings of an operation that is often opposed to representation, namely montage.

In his essay on 'Word and image' in *The Film Sense*, Eisenstein defines montage. Amongst numerous examples of montage he quotes the following from Ambrose Bierce's *Fantastic Fables*:

> A Woman in widow's weeds was weeping upon a grave.
> 'Console yourself, madam' said a Sympathetic Stranger.
> 'Heaven's mercies are infinite. There is another man somewhere, beside your husband, with whom you can still be happy.'
> 'There was,' she sobbed – 'there was, but this is his grave.'
> (Eisenstein 1968 14–15)

Eisenstein explains the effect of this fable in terms of an interaction between the visual representations in the story. The woman is a representation and so is the mourning dress – they are, in Eisenstein's terms, objectively representable – but the juxtaposition of these representations gives rise to a new image that is not representable – namely that the woman is a widow. It is the expectation created by the juxtaposition which is undercut by the final line uttered by the woman. For the moment we shall only notice the following point:

1 that Eisenstein, concerned very largely with a simple definition of representation, fails to recognise that widow is just as objective a representation as woman or mourning dress and

2 that montage involves both an interaction between representations and a shock.

Eisenstein continues his explanation by expanding his distinction between representation (the raw material of the montage) and image (that which is produced by the montage itself).

> Take a white circular disc of average size and smooth surface, its circumference divided into sixty equal parts. At every fifth division is set a figure in the order of succession of 1 to 12. At the centre of the disc are fixed two metal rods, moving freely on their fixed ends, pointed at their free ends, one being equal to the radius of the disc, the other rather shorter. Let the longer pointed rod have its free end resting at the figure 12 and the shorter in succession pointing towards the figures 1, 2, 3 and so on up to 12. This will comprise a series of geometrical representations of successive relations of the two metal rods to one another expressed in the dimensions 30, 60, 90 degrees, and so on up to 360 degrees.
>
> If, however, this disc is provided with a mechanism that imparts

steady movement to the metal rods, the geometrical figure formed on the surface acquires a special meaning: it is now not simply a *representation*, it is an *image* of time. (1968:20)

The confusion that led Eisenstein to count woman and mourning dress as representable but widow as non-representable can be seen at work again in this passage. Eisenstein thinks of the world as being composed of basic objects available to sight which are then linked together in various ways by the perceiving subject with the aid of his past experiences. That this is his position is made abundantly clear in the passage which follows the passage I have just quoted. He takes the example of Vronsky looking at his watch, after Anna Karenina has told him that she is pregnant, and being so shocked that he sees the position of the hands but not the time. Thus the position of the hands is the primitive object in the world and the time is what the human subject creates through his linking of this object with other items of his experience. Montage is thus, for Eisenstein, in this passage (which must not be confused with Eisenstein's cinematic practice), the manipulation of definite representations to produce images in the mind of the spectator. But now it can be seen that this definition of montage does not contradict representation at all. If we understand by representation the rendering of identities in the world then Eisenstein's account of montage is not opposed to representation but is simply a secondary process which comes after representation. Eisenstein would have montage linking onto representation but not in any sense challenging it. The representation starts from an identity in the world which it re-presents, the montage starts from representations, identities, and combines them to form an image.

Eisenstein's acceptance of representation can be seen in those passages where representation is contrasted with montage. For Eisenstein the opposite to montage is 'Affadavit-exposition' which he defines as '*in film terms; representations shot from a single set up*'. (1968:37) Thus montage is the showing of the same representation from different points of view. And it is from this point that we can begin to challenge Eisenstein's conception of montage. A point of view suggests two things. Firstly a view — something that is seen — and secondly a location from which the view may be had, the sight may be seen. Thus the suggestion is that there are different locations from which we can see. But in all cases the sight remains the same – the activity of representation is not the determining factor in the sight seen but simply the place from where it is seen. The inevitable result of this is that there is something the same which we all see but which appears differently because of our position. But if there is identity; if there is something over and above the views which can be received at different points then this identity must be discernable from some other 'point of view'. And this neutral point of view is exactly the 'representations shot from a single set-up'.

What is at work in Eisenstein's argument is the idea that there is some fixed reality which is available to us from an objective point of view (the single set-up). Montage is simply putting these fixed elements together in such a way that the subject brings forth other elements in his experience – but without any change in the identities, the elements that are being rendered. It is essential to realise that this account leaves both subject and object unchallenged and that montage becomes a kind of super-representation which is more effective at demonstrating the real qualities of the object through the links it can form within the subject. Thus Eisenstein would analyse the Bierce story as the representation of a given set of elements which are first organised in one way then in another. There are, however, no such set of fixed elements in the Bierce story. It is not that there is a set of elements which the reader composes 'in his mind' but rather that these elements are already determined by the method of representation. What Eisenstein ignores is that the method of representation (the language: verbal or cinematic) determines in its structural activity (the oppositions which can be articulated) both the places where the object 'appears' and the 'point' from which the object is seen. It is this point which is exactly the place allotted to the reading subject.

A careful analysis of the Bierce story may enable us to discover how montage operates and why that operation is difficult to grasp. We can read three different discourses at work in the Bierce story (a discourse being defined as a set of significant oppositions). The narrative discourse, the discourse of the Sympathetic Stranger and the discourse of the Woman. The question is whether as Eisenstein holds, the narrative discourse represents simply a woman and a mourning dress. But 'woman' is not some simple identity as Eisenstein would have us believe. Whereas the Sympathetic Stranger identifies woman in terms of religion and state – thus our relationships are determined in heaven and are institutionalised by the state on earth – the Woman determines her own identity as 'woman' in terms of desire and transgression – relationships are formed through the transgressing of the state's institutions and this transgression is linked with a certain sexuality; for relationships between a man and a woman outside the bond of holy matrimony are explicitly sexual. We can now understand that the montage works through a contest between the identities offered by the different discourses in the Bierce story, the woman's statement jars with what has gone before so that we re-read it – the identifications that we made (that were made for us) are undermined by new ones. What is thrown into doubt is exactly the identity (the nature) of woman and this doubt is achieved through the 'shock' of the woman's statement as the identity already proffered is subverted. It is also clear from this analysis that there is no neutral place from which we can see the view and where all the points are located. There is no possible language of 'affadavit-exposition' that would show the scene 'as it really is'. For how we see the scene will be determined by the way in which we identify 'woman' – and this determination is a feature of the available discourses; the discourses in which 'woman' can figure.

We are still, however, left with the problem of how we can mistake this effect of montage, as I have suggested Eisenstein has done, and the answer to this question can be found in the apparent similarity of the discourses in the Bierce story. For the three discourses are so similar that we can be persuaded to read them as one. All that is missing from the first and second is provided by the third. The third discourse can be read as 'closing' the text. For with the information thus given to us we can read the previous discourses in a 'final' – that is to say *once and for all* – manner. We can fill in the gaps in the first two discourses – see the real identities which are mistaken. But this is to ignore the fact that what is at question in the story are different discourses. Different discourses can be defined in discourses in which different oppositions are possible. Although at one level – the level of the legal relationship to the body and the grave – both discourses coincide (she *is* or *is not* the wife), at another level there are a set of oppositions of an emotional nature (she *does* or *does not* mourn some man) which the stranger cannot articulate outside the oppositions determined by the legal relationship. Bierce's story, through the coincidences between the discourses on one level, suggests to Eisenstein a set of identities in the world. But the identities rest in the discourses. Thus opposed to Eisenstein's concept of montage resting on the juxtapositions of identities already rendered, we could talk of montage as the effect generated by a conflict of discourse in which the oppositions available in the juxtaposed discourses are contradictory and in conflict.

All this by way of explaining that the classic realist text (a heavily 'closed' discourse) cannot deal with the real in its contradictions and that in the same movement it fixes the subject in a point of view from which everything becomes obvious. There is, however, a level of contradiction into which the classic realist text can enter. This is the contradiction between the dominant discourse of the text and the dominant ideological discourses of the time. Thus a classic realist text in which a strike is represented as a just struggle in which oppressed workers attempt to gain some of their rightful wealth would be in contradiction with certain contemporary ideological discourses and as such might be classified as progressive. It is here that subject matter enters into the argument and where we can find the justification for Marx and Engels's praise of Balzac and Lenin's texts on the revolutionary force of Tolstoy's texts which ushered the Russian peasant on to the stage of history. Within contemporary films one could think of the films of Costa-Gavras or such television documentaries as *Cathy Come Home*. What is, however, still impossible for the classic realist text is to offer any perspectives for struggle due to its inability to investigate contradiction. It is thus not surprising that these films tend either to be linked to a social democratic conception of progress – if we reveal injustices then they will go away – or certain *ouvrieriste* tendencies which tend to see the working class, outside any dialectical movement, as the simple possessors of truth. It is at this point that Brecht's demand that literary and artistic productions be regarded as social events gains its force. The contradictions between the dominant discourse in a classic realist text and the dominant ideological discourses at work in a society are what

44

provide the criteria for discriminating within the classic realist text. And these criteria will often resolve themselves into questions of subject-matter. That this tends to leave open any question about the eternal values of art is not something that should worry us. As Brecht remarks:

> To be frank, I do not set such an excessively high value on the concept of endurance. How can we foresee whether future generations will wish to preserve the memory of these figures [*figures created by Balzac or Tolstoy*]? (Balzac and Tolstoy will scarcely be in a position to oblige them to do so, however ingenious the methods with which they set their plots in motion.) I suspect it will depend on whether it will be a socially relevant statement if someone says: 'That' (and 'that' will refer to a contemporary) 'is a Père Goriot character'. Perhaps such characters will not survive? Perhaps they precisely arose in a cramping web of relations of a type which will no longer exist.[5]
>
> (XIX, 308–9)

Moments of subversion and strategies of subversion

> The practical methods of the revolution are not revolutionary, they are dictated by the class struggle. It is for this reason that great writers find themselves ill at ease in the class struggle, they behave as though the struggle was already finished, and they deal with the new situation, conceived as collectivist, which is the aim of the revolution. The revolution of the great writers is permanent.   (XVIII, 16)[6]

In the last issue of *Screen* we published Franco Fortini's text on 'The writer's mandate' (1974) which took the position that art is that area which deals with the irreconcilable contradictions of life over and beyond the particular contradictions of the class struggle and of their successful resolution in the revolution. It was suggested in the editorial that, in order to avoid a fall into romantic and ultra-left positions, these irreconcilable differences had to be theorised within the scientific concepts offered to us by psychoanalysis. Freud's theory is a theory of the construction of the subject: the entry of the small infant into language and society and the methods by which it learns what positions, as subject, it can take up. This entry into the symbolic (the whole cultural space which is structured, like language through a set of differences and oppositions) is most easily traced in the analytic situation through that entry which is finally determining for the infant – the problem of sexual difference. Freud's insight is that the unproblematic taking up of the position of the subject entails the repression of the whole mechanism of the subject's construction. The subject is seen as the founding source of meanings – unproblematically standing outside an articulation in which it is, in fact, defined. This view of the subject as founding source is philosophically encapsulated in Descartes' *cogito*: I think, therefore I am – the I in simple evidence to itself provides a moment of pure presence which can found the enterprise of analysing the world. Jacques Lacan, the French psychoanalyst, has read Freud as reformulating the Cartesian *cogito* and destroying the subject as source and foundation – Lacan rewrites the *cogito*, in the light of Freud's discoveries as, I think where I am not and I am where I do not think. We can understand this formulation as the indicating of the fundamental misunderstanding (*méconnaissance*) which is involved in the successful use of language (or any other area of the symbolic which is similarly structured) in which the subject is continually ignored as being caught up in a process of articulation to be taken as a fixed place founding the discourse. The unconscious is that effect of language which escapes the conscious subject in the distance between the act of signification in which the subject passes from signifier to signifier and what is signified in which the subject finds himself in place as, for example, the pronoun 'I'. The importance of phenomena like verbal slips is that they testify to the existence of the unconscious through the distance between what was said and what the conscious subject intended to say. They thus testify to the distance between the subject of the act of signification and the conscious subject (the ego). In this distance there is opened a gap which is the area of desire. What is essential to all of those psychic productions which Freud uses in the analytic interpretation is that they bear witness to the lack of control of the conscious subject over his discourses. The mechanisms of the unconscious can indeed be seen as the mechanisms of language. Condensation is the work of metaphor which brings together two signifieds under one signifier and displacement is the constant process along the signifying chain. The ego is constantly caught in this fundamental misunderstanding (*méconnaissance*) about language in which from an illusory present it attempts to read only one signified as present in the metaphor and attempts to bring the signifying chain to an end in a perpetually deferred present.

The relationship between the unconscious and desire, the subject and language is concisely summarised by Lacan in the following passage:

> There is not *an* unconscious because then there would be an unconscious desire which was obtuse, heavy, caliban like, even animal like, an unconscious desire lifted up from the depths which would be primitive and would have to educate itself to the superior level of consciousness. Completely on the contrary there is desire because there is unconsciousness (*de l'inconscient*) – that's to say language which escapes the subject in its structure and in its effects and there is always at the level of language something which is beyond consciousness and it is there that one can situate the function of desire.
>
> (Safouan 1968: 253)

It is clear that the classic realist text, as defined above, guarantees the position of the subject exactly outside any articulation – the whole text works on the concealing of the dominant discourse as articulation – instead the dominant discourse presents itself exactly as the presentation of objects to the reading subject. But within the classic realist text the dominant discourse can be subverted, brought into question – the position of the subject may be rendered problematic. If we return to our original example of George Eliot we can see this process of subversion at work in *Daniel Deronda*. Within the text there is a discourse, the writings of Mordecai in Hebrew, which are unmastered by the dominant discourse. The text tells us that they are untranslatable and thus that there is an area outside the text's control. This area is exactly the area of the mother-tongue (Daniel's mother is Jewish) and this mother-tongue subverts the assured positions of both the characters in the text and the reading subject. My business here is not to give a full analysis of George Eliot's work but rather to indicate the possibility of *moments* within a classical realist text which subvert it and its evident status for subject and object. We are relatively fortunate in already possessing this kind of analysis within the cinema in the *Cahiers du Cinéma*'s reading of John Ford's *Young Mr Lincoln*.[7] These *moments* are those elements which escape the control of the dominant discourse in the same way as a neurotic symptom or a verbal slip attest to the lack of control of the conscious subject. They open up another area than that of representation – of subject and object caught in an eternal paralysed fixity – in order to investigate the very movement of

47

articulation and difference – the movement of desire. (It is these moments which have been privileged by Roland Barthes and the *Tel Quel* group over the last few years and which have been theorised through the evaluative concept of text.) Over and above these *moments* of subversion, however, there are what one might call *strategies* of subversion. Instead of a dominant discourse which is transgressed at various crucial moments we can find a systematic refusal of any such dominant discourse. One of the best examples of a cinema which practices certain strategies of subversion are the films of Roberto Rossellini. In *Germany Year Zero*, for example, we can locate a multitude of ways in which the reading subject finds himself without a position from which the film can be regarded. Firstly, and most importantly, the fact that the narrative is not privileged in any way with regard to the characters' discourses. The narrative does not produce for us the knowledge with which we can then judge the truth of those discourses. Rather than the narrative providing us with knowledge – it provides us with various settings. Just as in Brecht the 'fable' serves simply as a procedure to produce the various *gests*, so in Rossellini the story simply provides a framework for various scenes which then constitute the picture of Germany in year zero. (It might be remarked that this unimportance of narrative is even more strongly marked in *Francesco Guillare di Dio*, where the device of introducing the various tableaux without narrative connection is more evident.) Indeed the narrative of *Germany Year Zero* can be seen as a device to introduce the final *gest* of Edmund's suicide – and in this it closely resembles the first reel of Brecht's own *Kuhle Wampe*. Secondly, Rossellini's narrative introduces many elements which are not in any sense resolved and which deny the possibility of regarding the film as integrated through a dominant discourse. The Allied soldiers, the street kids, the landlord, the Teacher's house – all these provide elements which stretch outside the narrative of the film and deny its dominance.

The result of these two strategies is that the characters themselves cannot be identified in any final way. Instead of their discourses, clothes, mannerisms being the punctual expressions of an identity fixed by the narrative – each element is caught up in a complex set of differences. The whole problematic of inside and outside which preoccupies the classic realist text is transformed

48

into a series of relationships in which word, dress, action and gesture interact to provide a never-finished series of significant differences which is the character.

It may be objected that it is deliberately perverse to tear Rossellini away from realism with which he has been firmly connected both through his own statements and through critical reception. The realist element in Rossellini is not simply located in the subject matter, the traditional criterion of realism, for I have already argued that the subject matter is a secondary condition for realism. What typifies the classic realist text is the way the subject matter is ordered and articulated rather than its origins. To deal with the facts of the world is, in itself, not only a realist but also a materialist viewpoint. The materialist, however, must regard these materials as ordered within a certain mode of production, within which they find their definition. And it is here that one could begin to isolate that element of realist ideology which does figure in Rossellini's films as a certain block. If the reading subject is not offered any certain mode of entry into what is presented on the screen, he is offered a certain mode of entry to the screen itself. For the facts presented by the camera, if they are not ordered in fixed and final fashion amongst themselves, *are* ordered in themselves. The camera, in Rossellini's films is not articulated as part of the productive process of the film. What it shows is in some sense beyond argument and it is here that Rossellini's films show the traditional realist weakness of being unable to deal with contradiction. In *Viva l'Italia* the glaring omission of the film is the absence of Cavour. It is wrong to attack this omission on purely political grounds for it is an inevitable result of a certain lack of questioning of the camera itself. Garibaldi can be contrasted with Francisco II of Naples because their different conceptions of the world are so specifically tied to different historical eras that the camera can cope with their contradictions within an historical perspective. Here is the way the world is now – there is the way the world was then. But to introduce Cavour would involve a simultaneous contradiction – a class contradiction. At this point the camera itself, as a neutral agent, would become impossible. For it would have to offer two present contradictory articulations of the world and thus reveal its own presence. This cannot happen within a Rossellini film where if we are continually aware of our presence

49

in the cinema (particularly in his historical films) – that presence itself is not questioned in any way. We are not allowed any particular position to read the film but we are allowed the position of a reader – an unproblematic viewer – an eternally human nature working on the material provided by the camera.

A possible way of advancing on Rossellini's practice (there are no obvious films which have marked such an advance although some of Godard's early films might be so considered) would be to develop the possibility of articulating contradiction. Much in the way that James Joyce in *Ulysses* and *Finnegans Wake* investigated the contradictory ways of articulating reality through an investigation of the different forms of language, one could imagine a more radical strategy of subversion than that practised by Rossellini in which the possibilities of the camera would be brought more clearly into play. What would mark such a cinema and indeed any cinema of subversion would be that feature quoted by Brecht at the beginning of this section – the fact that it would be ill at ease in the class struggle, always concerned with an area of contradiction beyond the necessity of the present revolution – the ineliminable contradictions of the sexes, the eternal struggle between Desire and Law, between articulation and position.

A possible category: the revolutionary text

Socialist emulation forms individuals in a different way and produces different individuals. Then there is the further question whether it is anyway as individuating a process as the capitalist competitive struggle. (XIX,310)[8]

It is precisely this sharp opposition between work and leisure, which is peculiar to the capitalist mode of production, that separates all intellectual activity into those activities which serve work and those activities which serve leisure. And those that serve leisure organised into a system for the reproduction of the labour force. Distractions must not contain anything which is contained in work. Distractions, in the interest of production, are committed to non-production. Naturally, it is not thus that one can create a style of life which forms a unique and coherent whole. And this cannot be put down to the fact that art is dragged into the productive process, but to the fact that it is incompletely involved in the productive process and that it must create an island of 'non-production'. The man who buys a ticket transforms himself in front of the screen into an idier and an exploiter (*Ausbeuter*). Since booty (*Beute*) is placed within him here he is as it were a victim of im-ploitation (*Einbeutung*). (XVIII, 169).[9]

In his article in *Screen* 15, 2 (1974), Roland Barthes suggests that revolutionary artists such as Eisenstein and Brecht must, of necessity, remain within the world of representation. Barthes throughout his article uses the structure of fetishism as his model for the structure of representation. Stephen Heath's article in the same issue investigates this comparison at length but it might be useful to indicate briefly the importance of the concept of fetishism. The fetish is that object which places the subject in a position of security outside of that terrifying area of difference opened up by the perception of the mother's non-possession of the phallus. Although most popular accounts of fetishism concentrate on the fetishised objects, it is exemplary for Barthes as a structure which holds both subject and object in place – it is the fetish above all that holds the subject in position. What is essential to Barthes's argument is the idea that the subject must always be the same – caught in the same position vis-à-vis the world. Within this view a revolutionary work of art can do no more than provide a correct representation (provided by the Party) of the world. It may be helpful to attain this goal to subvert the position of the subject so that his acceptance of the new representation is facilitated but finally the revolutionary artist is committed (condemned) to the world of representation.

Within the framework I have constructed in this article one could say that the revolutionary artist may practice certain strategies of subversion but must finally content himself with the production of a progressive realist text. The question I want to raise here, and it must be emphasised that it can only be raised, is the possibility of *another* activity which rather than the simple subversion of the subject or the representation of different (and *correct*) identities, would consist of the displacement of the subject within ideology – a different constitution of the subject. It has been accepted, particularly over the last ten years in France, that the subject is the crucial concept for a Marxist theory of ideology – a theory which would attempt to explain the non-coercive ways in which the capitalist mode of production ensures the reproduction of labour power and would also attempt to furnish guidelines for the practical tasks in the question of changing

51

ideology – the whole problem of the cultural revolution. One of the difficulties of using the subject as such a key term is that it is an ideological notion which is willy-nilly transformed into a descriptive scientific concept. The sub-ject – that which under-lies experience – is a production, very largely, of modern European philosophy from Descartes to its most sophisticated articulation in the philosophers of German Idealism.

The main problem facing anyone wishing to articulate a theory of film with a Marxist theory of ideology is that by and large no such Marxist theory exists. Marx never really returned to the subject after 1846 and none of the other great Marxist theoreticians (with the possible exception of Gramsci) have found the time to devote themselves to the problem. In many ways the starting point of any such investigation must be Louis Althusser's essay on the topic entitled 'Ideology and ideological state apparatuses (Notes towards an investigation)' (1971). In this essay Althusser puts forward and defends the thesis that ideology has no history. By this he does not mean that specific ideologies do not have a history involving both internal and external factors but that the very form of ideology is always the same. Althusser argues that the central and unvarying feature of ideology is that it represents the imaginary relationship of individuals to their real conditions of existence. Ideology is always 'imaginary' because these representations place the subject in position in his society. In other words ideology always has a place for a founding source outside the real articulations.

Before discussing this thesis directly there are two preliminary points that must be made, which while they do not touch directly on the thesis need to be borne in mind when discussing it. The first, which I have already touched on, is that the subject is an ideological notion. Moreover, it is an ideological notion which is tied very closely to the rise of the bourgeoisie. It would be outside the scope of this article and beyond the author's competence to trace the evolution of this notion with any precision. Suffice to say that Cartesian philosophy, Newtonian physics and the grammar of Port-Royal all involve very precisely that notion of a unified subject of experience and that the birth of this notion in the seventeenth century suggests very important links with the growing economic and political domination of the European bourgeoisie – the works of Locke provide perhaps the most obvious example of the need for this category of subject in the justification both of the new science and the new civil order.[10] All this simply by way of a warning of the difficulties of dealing with the notion of the subject.

Secondly it is necessary to realise what an important break Althusser's thesis marks with certain methods of Hegelianising Marx. For Althusser is concerned to attack that view which, seeing ideology as 'merely' illusory, holds out the promise that the victorious conclusion to the class struggle will result in the arrival of the new and true ideology which will correspond to the real. This view merely incarnates the Hegelian version that being and consciousness will finally coincide within a simple view of the end of class struggle. It is the proletariat that will realise the beautiful dream of the real becoming rational and the rational becoming real. Whatever reservations one may have about Althusser's thesis, it is important that they do not involve a slipping back into such a Hegelian model with all the lack of contradiction and struggle that it implies.

To return, however, directly to Althusser's thesis. It seems an inevitable result of this thesis that art can be allotted no specific field of action other than its effects on the content of ideology. As such art remains firmly within the realm of ideology, being simply one of a number of internal factors within the evolution of ideologies. This is, of course, quite compatible with classical Marxist positions on art, but traditional Marxist thought has often felt itself embarrassed by this simple lumping of art into ideology — one of the most famous examples of such an embarrassment is Marx's own attempt to deal with the problem of Greek art. There is, however, another way in which this problem can be approached and it is suggested by Brecht's remark on the position of the spectator in the cinema (quoted at the beginning of this section) and by much of Brecht's theory and practice. Here one would have to deny both Althusser's (and Marx's) thesis that ideology has no history and at the same time delimit a special area of activity which is neither that of science nor that of ideology. This activity might be characterised by its ability actually to work on and transform the very form of ideology — to change the position of the subject within ideology.

What Brecht suggests in his comments on the spectator in the cinema is that the very position offered to the spectator is one that guarantees the necessary re-production of labour power. It is the cinema's ability to place the spectator in the position of a unified subject that ensures the contradiction between his working activity which is productive and the leisure activity in which he is constantly placed as consumer. Althusser makes the very important point in his essay that ideology is not a question of ideas circulating in people's heads but is inscribed in certain material practices. The reactionary practice of the cinema is that which involves this petrification of the spectator in a position of pseudo-dominance offered by the metalanguage. This meta-language, resolving as it does all contradictions, places the spectator outside the realm of contradiction and of action – outside of production.

Two films which suggest a way of combating this dominance of the metalanguage, without falling into an agnostic position vis-à-vis all discourses (which would be the extreme of a subversive cinema – intent merely on disrupting any position of the subject) are *Kuhle Wampe* (the film in which Brecht participated) and Godard-Gorin's *Tout Va Bien*. In both films the narrative is in no way privileged as against the characters. Rather the narrative serves simply as the method by which various situations can be articulated together. The emphasis is on the particular scenes and the knowledge that can be gained from them rather than the providing of a knowledge which requires no further activity – which just is there on the screen. Indeed the presentation of the individual's discourses is never stripped away from the character's actions but is involved in them. Whether it is a question of the petit-bourgeois and the workers discussing the waste of coffee in the S-Bahn or the various monologues in *Tout Va Bien* – it is not a question of the discourses being presented as pure truth content which can be measured against the truth provided by the film. Rather the discourses are caught up in certain modes of life which are linked to the place of the agent in the productive process. The unemployed workers know that waste is an inevitable part of the capitalist process because they experience it every day in their search for work. Equally the workers in the meat factory know that the class struggle is not finished for they experience the exploitation of their labour in such concrete details as the time that is allowed them to go to the toilet. The film does not provide this knowledge ready-made in a dominant discourse but in the contradictions offered, the reader has to produce a meaning for the film (it is quite obvious in films of this sort that the meaning produced will depend on the class-positions of the reader). It is this emphasis on the reader as producer (more obvious in *Tout Va Bien* which is in many ways more Brechtian than *Kuhle Wampe*) which suggests that these films do not just offer a different representation for the subject but a different set of relations to both the fictional material and 'reality'.

Very briefly this change could be characterised as the introduction of time (history) into the very area of representation so that it is included within it. It is no accident that both films end with this same emphasis on time and its concomitant change. 'But who will change the world' (*Kuhle Wampe*) – 'We must learn to live historically' (*Tout Va Bien*) – this emphasis on time and change embodied both within the film and in the position offered to the reader suggests that a revolutionary socialist ideology might be different in form as well as content. It also throws into doubt Barthes's thesis that revolutionary art is finally caught in the same space of representation that has persisted for 2,000 years in the West. This monolithic conception of representation ignores the fact that post-Einsteinian physics offers a conception of representation in which both subject and object are no longer caught in fixed positions but caught up in time.

It might be thought that this possibility of change, of transformation – in short, of production – built into the subject-object relation (which could no longer be characterised in this simple fashion) simply reduplicates the Hegelian error of final reconciliation between the orders of being and consciousness. But this is not so in so far as this possibility of change built into the relation does not imply the inevitable unfolding of a specific series of changes but simply the possibility of change – an area of possible transformations contained within the relation.

It seems that some such account must be offered if one wishes to allow the possibility of a revolutionary art. Otherwise it seems inevitable that art can simply be progressive or subversive and Brecht's whole practice would be a marriage of the two, in which subversive effects were mechanically used simply to aid the acceptance of the progressive content of his work.

Theoretical essays

A definite category: reactionary art

> It is our metaphysicians of the press, our partisans of 'art' who would like more emphasis on 'fate' in human processes. For a long time now fate, which was once a sublime notion, has been nothing more than a mediocre received idea: by reconciling himself to his condition, man arrives at that so longed for 'transfiguration' and 'interiorisation'. It is equally a pure notion of the class struggle: one class 'determines' the fate of the other.   (XVII, 169–70)[11]

One fashionable way of receiving and recuperating Brecht, which has been at work since the beginning of the Cold War, is to see him as a satirist ridiculing his contemporary society and the excesses of capitalism and fascism. This approach negates the productive element in Brecht's work and turns the techniques for the production of alienation effects into pure narcissistic signals of an 'intellectual' work of 'art'. A very typical example of this vulgarisation and de-politicisation of Brecht can be seen in Lindsay Anderson's *O Lucky Man!* An explicitly Brechtian film – the loosely connected scenes are counter-pointed by the Alan Price songs – the film pretends to offer a tableau of England in 1973 much as *Tout Va Bien* attempts to offer a tableau of France in 1972. But whereas in the French film the tableaux are used to reflect the contradictions within the society – the different articulations of reality – in the English film the tableaux are all used to express a stereotyped reality of England which the spectator is invited to enjoy from his superior position. The scenes may seem to be dominant over the reality revealed by the narrative but as the film progresses along its endless development it becomes obvious that the narrative simply confirms the evident truths which are offered to us on the screen. And these truths turn out to be that endless message of the reactionary petit-bourgeois intellectual – that we can do nothing against the relentless and evil progress of society (run as it is by a bunch of omnipotent capitalists with the morality of gangsters) except note our superiority to it. A longer analysis of the film might well be in order were it not for the fact that Walter Benjamin had already written the definitive critique of this particularly impoverished artistic strategy. It is perhaps a testament to the paucity of petit-bourgeois imagination in the era of monopoly capitalism that what Benjamin wrote forty years ago about the satirical poet Erich Kästner (1974)can be applied word for word to *O Lucky Man!*

Notes

1. SC p. 93. For explanation of annotation used for Brecht's works see note 2.
2. If the quotation is from Brecht then I simply give the volume and page number of the German edition (1967) in the text and the French page numbers which are taken from the volumes published in 1970 as *Sur le Réalisme* (SR) and *Sur le Cinéma* (SC) in the footnotes. If the piece was included in the translations of Brecht in issue 84 of *New Left Review* then I add a third figure after the initials NLR.
3. SR p. 98, NLR p. 45.
4. SR p. 77.
5. SR pp. 99–100, NLR p. 46.
6. SC p. 25.
7. *Screen* 13, 3, Autumn 1972.
8. SR p. 101, NLR p. 47.
9. SC pp. 178–9.
10. This precise locating of the notion of the subject in the seventeenth century can, of course, be contested. Althusser, himself, uses examples from the Christian religion and from the Pentateuch which accords with his view of the category of the subject as eternal within ideology. All I wish to indicate in this passage is that it is not obvious that the category of the subject can be used with the degree of confidence that Althusser assumes.
11. SC p. 179.

Theory and film: principles of realism and pleasure

Introduction

Film theory has undergone an extraordinary expansion and mutation in the last few years. Without wishing to specify either their relative importance or their interdependence, one could indicate three factors which have contributed to this growth: increasingly heterogenous developments within filmic practice; an enlarged educational investment; and a growing concern with the general theoretical problems of signification. The result of these complex determinants is that, while developing its own specific area of analysis, film theory has come in recent years to have more and more to contribute to many of the most important and central cultural debates. *Screen* has participated actively in this process and it is through a consideration of one crucial area of discussion, namely realism, that we can attempt to understand the impetus and direction of *Screen*'s work in the recent past. Brecht remarked that realism was not simply a matter for aesthetic debate but was one of the crucial questions of our age. The problems of realism occur in an acute and critical form in the cinema and perhaps no single topic concentrates so many of the developments that have taken place in film theory.

If we say that realism is, and has been, the dominant aesthetic in film, it is important to realise that this dominance does not date from film's inception. At the moment of its invention, various possibilities remained open to film; possibilities which were closed down by a set of ideological choices, and the manner of this closure is of great interest to the study of ideology. But if we recognise the extent to which realism became dominant in film only after the development of sound, and after film production

58

throughout the world had been hegemonised in Hollywood, it is still the case that realism has been the dominant aesthetic since the Second World War. Whether we look at Hollywood, where realism is purchased at almost any price, or to the Italian neo-realist cinema, we find that the struggle is to represent reality as effectively as possible; in both cinemas the possibility as such of the representational relation is taken for granted. If cinéma-vérité opposed Hollywood, this opposition was in terms of the effacement of style, where a pristine representation, an authentic relation between film and fact, was contaminated by arrangement and conscious intervention. Only in the early 1960s do we begin to find filmic practices which question the very validity of the representational relation. Within the continental tradition, and owing an explicit debt to neo-realism and particularly to Rossellini, the films of Godard began an investigation of film which took as its object the very process of representation as well as the problem of what was represented. At the same time, in America, the development of cheaper film-making technology allowed many of the theoretical concerns of modern American painting to find a practical application in film. The name of Warhol can serve as an index of this development. But if these practices can best be articulated outside any representational problematic, the theoretical debates around them have constantly lagged behind those practices and, very often, the most important factor contributing to this backwardness has been difficulties with the problem of realism. At the same time a traditional realism remains the dominant force within the commercial cinema, where, if many of the tricks and effects of other cinemas are constantly borrowed, films like *Nashville* or *American Graffiti* reproduce the major strategies and procedures of films like *Giant* or *The Chase*. Finally, realism poses a constant problem within the Marxist theoretical and political tradition as a legacy of the primacy attached to it in the Soviet Union in the 1930s. It is thus difficult in any field of cinema to avoid the term and indeed it is vitally necessary to examine it and its consequences in some detail.

Realism and empiricism
As a starting point one could take the objection that realism cannot be dominant in the cinema because Hollywood cinema is not

realistic. By the criteria of one of the great realist critics, André Bazin, for a film to be realistic, it must locate its characters and action in a determinate social and historical setting. Most Hollywood films, it could be argued, fail to do this and are, therefore, unrealistic. But Bazin's characterisation of realism is much more centrally concerned with a transparency of form which is reduplicated within Hollywood filmic practice. Bazin's criteria for distinguishing between films can only be based on non-filmic concerns. (It should be said in advance that although these considerations will tend to collapse Hollywood and neo-realist cinema together, there is a different reading of Bazin which could disengage from his text a set of incoherences which can be articulated so as to produce distinctions between neo-realism and much Hollywood cinema such that the value judgements Bazin wished to confer on the post-war Italian cinema could be retained without out a commitment to Bazin's theory of representation.)[1]

For Bazin, as for almost all realist theorists, what is in question is not just a rendering of reality but the rendering of a reality made more real by the use of aesthetic device. Talking of the use of convention within the cinema, Bazin writes that such a use may be made

> at the service or at the disservice of realism, it may increase˙ or neutralise the efficacity of the elements of reality captured by the camera ... One can class, if not hierarchise, the cinematographic styles as a function of the gain of reality that they represent. We shall thus call *realist* any system of expression, any narrative procedure which tends to make more reality appear on the screen.
>
> (Bazin 1962: 22)

This 'more' is not quantitative but qualitative: it measures the extent to which the essence of the object represented is grasped. For Bazin the essence is attained through globality and totality; it is understood as coherence. Rossellini's version is assessed in terms of the globality of the real that it represents: this globality

> does not signify, completely the contrary, that neo-realism can be reduced to some objective documentaryism. Rossellini likes to say that the basis of his conception of mise-en-scène lies in a love not only of his characters but also of reality just as it is and it is exactly this love which forbids him to dissociate that which reality has united; the character and the decor. Neo-realism is defined neither by a refusal

to take up a position with regard to the world nor by a refusal to judge it but it supposes in fact a mental attitude; it is always reality seen through an artist, refracted by his consciousness, but by all his consciousness, and not by his reason or his passion or his belief and reconstituted from dissociated elements   (1962: 154)

The central nature of the artistic activity becomes the presentation of a reality more real than that which could be achieved by a simple recording. The play on the notions of 'real' and 'reality' which is involved in Bazin's conception (the artist produces a reality more real than reality) is also the central feature of empiricism. In *Reading Capital*, Louis Althusser locates the specific feature of empiricism not in the confrontation between subject and object which is postulated as anterior to any knowledge (though to be sure empiricism relies on this), but rather in its characterisation of the knowledge to be obtained as defined by the object of which it is knowledge. Althusser writes: 'The whole empiricist process of knowledge lies in that operation of the subject named abstraction. To know is to abstract from the real object its essence, the possession of which by the subject is then called knowledge.' (1970: 35 – 6) The whole empiricist conception thus depends on two notions of real and ultimately two notions of object and this play suppresses the process at work in the production of knowledge. Bazin too starts out with the reality of everyday life and ends up with the greater reality of the film-maker's representation of it. What must be hidden by the 'author' is the process by which this 'greater reality' is arrived at, for, of course, on this account the 'greater reality' is there all along just waiting to be seen. Thus, for Bazin, any concept of process which would call both subject and object into play instead of positing them as constitutive moments is eliminated. This finds clear expression in his discussion of de Sica's *Bicycle Thieves*:

> As the disappearance of the actor is the result of an overcoming of the style of acting, the disappearance of the mise-en-scène is equally the fruit of a dialectical process of the style of narration. If the event is sufficient unto itself without the director having need to illuminate it by angles or the special position of the camera, it is that it has come to that perfect luminosity which permits art to unmask a nature which finally resembles it.   (1962: 57)

All interference by the subject must be reduced to a minimum because such interference involves subject and object in a process which destroys their full and punctual autonomy. The triumph of *Bicycle Thieves* is that it completely does away with the cinematic process. Bazin writes: '*Bicycle Thieves* is one of the first examples of pure cinema. There are no more actors, no more story, no more mise-en-scène, that is to say finally in the aesthetic illusion of reality – no more cinema' (1962: 59). The revelation of reality is the prime task of the cinema and all aesthetic devices are simply there to unmake themselves so that we too can experience, as the artist experienced before us, that moment at which reality presents itself as whole.

Contradiction and the real

Against this traditional analysis, I argue that film does not reveal the real in a moment of transparency, but rather that film is constituted by a set of discourses which (in the positions allowed to subject and object) produce a certain reality. The emphasis on production must be accompanied by one on another crucial Marxist term, that of contradiction. There is no one discourse that produces a certain reality – to believe so is to fall into the idealism complementary to the empiricism already discussed. A film analysis is dealing with a set of contradictory discourses transformed by specific practices. Within a film text these may be different 'views' of reality which are articulated together in different ways. Most documentaries bind the images together by the verbal interpretation of the voice-over commentary. Classical fictional cinema, on the other hand, has the crucial opposition between spoken discourses which may be mistaken and a visual discourse which guarantees truth – which reveals all. For this opposition to be set up, the spectator must be placed in a position from which the image is regarded as primary. The movement of this placing can be grasped by considering a third group of films which find their constitutive principle in the refusal so to place the spectator. In a film such as the Dziga-Vertov Group's *Wind from the East* a set of political discourses and images are juxtaposed so that, although what the Second Female Voice says is what the film-makers regard as politically correct, it neither subdues the images, as in the documentary, nor is judged by them. None of the discourses can be read off one against the other.

There is no possibility of verification, no correspondence between sound and image enabling the spectator to enter the realm of truth. This dislocation between sound and image focuses attention on the position of the spectator – both in the cinema and politically. These juxtapositions make the spectator constantly aware of the discourses that confront him as discourses – as, that is, the production of sets of positions – rather than allowing him to ignore the process of articulation by entering a world of correspondence in which the only activity required is to match one discourse against the realm of truth.

It might here be objected that 'filmic discourse' has not been defined with sufficient precision. Rather than giving an exact definition, one must indicate the range of application of the term. Within language studies, from at least the Renaissance onwards, discourse is the term used to indicate a shifting of attention from the formal oppositions which the linguist attempts to define and articulate to the way in which these formal oppositions relate to the speaking subject. When we talk of 'discourse' we move away from a conception of language as a set of significant oppositions independent of the speaking subject (Saussure's *langue*) to focus on the position of the speaking subject within the utterance. With discourse we become interested in the dialectical relation between speaker and language in which language always already offers a position to the speaker and yet, at the same time, the act of speaking may itself displace those positions. In filmic terms this means the kinds of combinations of words and images which can be differentiated in terms of different positions allocated to the viewer. I hope to make clear the kind of elements involved in this combination later in my examination of *American Graffiti*. For the moment it can be stated that it is neither a question of the film-maker using a transparent discourse to render the real nor of her or him inventing a discourse which produces a real. Instead the production of a film must be understood as involving a work, a practice, a transformation on and of the discourses available. One such practice, which I have called classical realism, and shall analyse in *American Graffiti*, involves the homogeneisation of different discourses by their relation to one dominant discourse – assured of its domination by the security and transparency of the image. The fact that one such practice involves this homogeneisation is a matter of ideological and political but not normative interest. My aim in this article is to demonstrate how the practices which articulate the different elements in the discourses which constitute a filmic text have certain political effects. For the moment, and against a traditional realist emphasis, one could say that, at any given time, it is the contradictory positions available discursively to the subject, together with the positions made available by non-linguistic practices, that constitute the reality of the social situation.

It is contradiction that Bazin wishes at all costs to conceal and coherence that furnishes him with his crucial emphasis. The coherence and the totality of the artist's vision provide the final criterion of reality – subject and object confront one another in full luminosity. This luminosity draws attention to the fact that the relation is visual – that all we have to do in the cinema is look. It is here that we begin to analyse the practices of classical realist cinema, for the distinguishing feature of these practices is the production of a perfect point of view for the audience – a point of vision.

The point of view and the look

Jacques Lacan has offered an analysis of vision which is of great relevance to any attempt to understand the reality of film. For Lacan, vision offers a peculiarly privileged basis to an *imaginary* relation of the individual to the world. This imaginary relationship is characterised by the plenitude it confers on both subject and object, caught as they are outside any definition in terms of difference – given in a full substantial unity. The imaginary is central to the operations of the human psyche and is constituted as such in early infancy. Somewhere between the sixth and eighteenth month, the small human infant discovers its reflection in the mirror; an apprehension of unity all the more surprising in that it normally occurs before motor control has ensured that unity in practice. The specular relation thus established in this, the mirror phase, provides the basis for primary narcissism, and is then transferred onto the rest of the human world where the other is simply seen as another version of the same – of the 'I' which is the centre of the world. It is only with the apprehension of genital difference that the child leaves the comfortable world of the imaginary to enter into the world of the symbolic. The symbolic is understood by Lacan (after Lévi-Strauss) not as a set of one-to-one relationships but as a tissue of differences which articulate the crucial elements within the child's world. it is the acceptance of a potential lack (castration) which marks the child's access to the symbolic and to language. Language in the realm of the imaginary is understood in terms of some full relation between word and thing; a mysterious unity of sign and referent. In the symbolic, language is understood in terms of lack and absence – the sign finds its definition diacritically through the absent syntagmatic and paradigmatic chains it enters into. As speaking subjects we constantly oscillate between the symbolic and the imaginary – constantly imagining ourselves granting some full meaning to the words we speak, and constantly being surprised to find them determined by relations outside our control. But if it is the phallus which is the determining factor for the entry into difference, difference has already troubled the full world of the infant. The imaginary unity has already been disrupted by the cruel separation from those objects originally understood as part of the subject – the breast and the faeces. The phallus becomes the dominating metaphor for all these previous lacks. Lacan defines the centrality of the phallus for the entry into the symbolic and language when he describes the phallus as 'the signifier destined to designate the effects, taken as a set, of signified, in so far as the signifier conditions these effects by its presence as signifier' (Lacan 1966:690). The signified here is exactly the imaginary full meaning constantly contaminated by the signifier's organisation along constitutive and absent chains.

In *Le Séminaire* XI, Lacan attempts to demonstrate the relation between the symbolic and the imaginary at the level of vision and to demonstrate the existence of lack within the scopic field (this lack being the condition of the existence of desire within the visual field – a desire which can find satisfaction in a variety of forms). Taking the Holbein picture 'The Ambassadors' (The National Gallery, London), Lacan comments on the death's head hidden in the picture by a trick of perspective and only visible from onc particular angle. The rest of the picture is caught in the world of the imaginary – the spectator is the all-seeing subject and, as if to emphasise the narcissistic nature of the relation, Holbein fills the picture with Renaissance emblems of vanity. However, the death's head, perceived when leaving the field of the picture, re-introduces the symbolic. For the death's head

65

draws attention to the fact that we see the picture at a distance and from a particular angle (if we think back to Bazin's quote about *Bicycle Thieves*, it is clear that for him cinema must obliterate distance and angles). With the introduction of the spectator's position the objects simply and substantially there are transformed into a set of differential relationships; a set of traces left by a paint brush; an organised area of space which, from one particular point, can be read as an object. That the object thus seen is a skull is in no way surprising when we consider that the entry into the symbolic can be most simply described as the recognition of the world independently of my consciousness – as the recognition, that is, of the possibility of my own death. Holbein's picture demonstrates a congruence between the organisation of language and the organisation of the visual field. Just as the constitutive elements of language must be absent in the moment of speaking, so the constitutive nature of the distance and position of the viewing subject must be absent from the all-embracing world of vision. 'The Ambassadors' re-introduces the look into vision. As such it bears witness to the separation (castration) on which vision is based, but which it endlessly attempts to ignore.

The intervention of the symbolic in the imaginary is already in evidence at the very opening of the mirror-phase. For the infant verifies its reflection by looking to the mother who holds it in front of the mirror. It is the mother's look that confirms the validity of the infant's image and with this look we find that at the very foundation of the dual imaginary relationship there is a third term already unsettling it. The mother verifies the relationship for the child, but at the cost of introducing a look, a difference where there should only be similitude. The fact that this look which both sets up and potentially destroys the full visual field is felt as castration explains why, traditionally, the eye is always evil. We are now in a position to grasp Lacan's claim that the visual is organised in terms of the look (*le regard*) – defined by the others' look that it is not – and of the blot (*la tache*), the fact that any visual field is already structured so that certain effects will be seen, Lacan writes: 'The function of the blot and the look is, at one and the same time, that which commands the most secretly, and that which always escapes the grip of, that form of vision which finds its contentment in imagining itself as consciousness' (Lacan 1973: 71).

Bazin wishes to do away with the camera because it constantly threatens the world of imaginary plenitude and must therefore be repressed at all costs. In its place a visual world is instituted from which the look, any trace of castration, has been expelled. The distinction between the symbolic and the imaginary can be understood in cinematic terms by contrasting the look and the point of view. The point of view is always related to an object (see Edward Branigan: 'Formal Permutations of the Point-of-View Shot,' *Screen* 16, 3, autumn 1975, pp. 54–64). But in so far as the object is a given unity there is always the possibility of seeing it together with all the possible points of view – there is always the possibility of a point of over-view. The point of view preserves the primacy of vision, for what is left out of one point-of-view shot can always be supplied by another. The look, however, is radically defective. Where the point of view is related to an object, the look is related to other looks. The look's field is not defined by a science of optics in which the eye features as a geometrical point, but by the fact that the object we are looking at offers a position from which we can be looked at – and this look is not punctual but shifts over the surface. It is important that it is a head that looks back at us from Holbein's painting.

From this account of the pleasure involved in vision it might seem that the ideal film would show us a static perspective. But this is to ignore the dialectic of pleasure and desire revealed to us by Freud. If, on the one hand, there is a tendency towards stasis, towards a normalisation of excitation within the psyche, there is also a compulsion to repeat those moments at which the stasis is set in motion, at which the level of excitation rises to unbearable heights. The small boy in *Beyond the Pleasure Principle* in his endless game of *fort-da*, ceaselessly throws away the object at the end of the string only to draw it back and start again. This action, which Freud tells us reproduces the experience of separation from the mother, shows that it is exactly the moment of anxiety, of heightened tension, the moment of coming which is relived in a constant cycle, which threatens life itself. What lies beyond the pleasure principle is not a threatening and exterior reality but a reality whose virulence knows no cessation, the reality of those constitutive moments at which we experience ourselves in the very moment of separation; which moments we are compelled to repeat in that endless movement which can find satisfaction only in death. Desire is only set up by absence, by the possibility of return to a former state — the field of vision only becomes invested libidinally after it has been robbed of its unity by the gaze of the other. The charm of classical realism is that it introduces the gaze of the other but this introduction is always accompanied by the guarantee of the supremacy of the point of view; the threat appears so that it can be smoothed over and it is in that smoothing that we can locate pleasure — in a plenitude which is fractured but only on condition that it will be re-set. Here the stock terms demonstrate what is at stake: the motion pictures, the movies, the flicks; it is the threat of motion, of displacement that is in question, but this threat is overcome from the start.

The logic of this contradictory movement can be understood on the basis of the set of interchanges that take place between screen and viewer — that complicated circulation which ensures that I am not only a spectator in the cinema but also, by a process of identification, a character on the screen. The cinema constantly poses me as the constant point of a fixed triangle and it constantly obscures and effaces the complicated progress of the shots, the impossible movements of that point by the logic of events on the screen. To analyse this process we need the concepts elaborated by Benveniste to distinguish betweent the *sujet de l'énonciation* and the *sujet de l'énoncé*. Benveniste suggests that to arrive at a logical understanding of tenses and to understand fully the importance of language for subjectivity, the speaker as the producer of the discursive chain, *le sujet de l'énonciation*, must be distinguished from the speaker as the grammatical subject, *le sujet de l'énoncé*. The distance between these two subjects gives us a formal linguistic account of the distance between the philosophical subject, *le sujet de l'énoncé*, the 'I', judge of the correspondence between world and language, and the psychoanalytic subject, the *sujet de l'énonciation*, the 'it', unable to distinguish between word and world and constantly threatening and unmasking the stability of the 'I'. Applied to film this is the distinction between the spectator as viewer, the comforting 'I', the fixed point, and the spectator as he or she is caught up in the play of events on the screen, as he or she 'utters', 'enounces' the film. Hollywood cinema is largely concerned to make these two coincide so that we can ignore what is at risk. But this coincidence can never be perfect because it is exactly in the divorce between the two that the film's existence is possible. This bringing into play of the process of the text's production takes us out of the classical field of semiotics, the field of the *énoncé* in which the text is treated as the assertion of a set of disjunctions permuted to produce actions, and into the question of the production of these very disjunctions. The subject is neither the full presence of traditional 'auteur' criticism nor the effect of the structure of traditional structuralism; it is divided in the movement between the two. The contradiction between *énonciation* and *énoncé* is also the contradiction between narrative and discourse. Narrative is always propelled by both a heterogeneity and a surplus − a heterogeneity which must be *both* overcome *and* prolonged. The narrative begins with an incoherence but already promises the resolution of that incoherence. The story is the passage from ignorance to knowledge, but this passage is denied as process − the knowledge is always already there as the comforting resolution of the broken coherence (every narration is always a suspense story). Narrative must deny the time of its own telling − it must refuse its status as discourse (as articulation), in favour of its self-presentation as simple identity, complete knowledge.

'American Graffiti': an example[2]

To understand a film like *American Graffiti*, its reality and its pleasure − the reality of its pleasure, it is necessary to consider the logic of that contradiction which produces a position for the viewer but denies that production. To admit that production would be to admit of position, and the position that has been produced is the position of the point of view, promising, as Bazin wished, that the event is sufficient to itself and needs no illumination from angles or the special position of the camera − promising, in short, a supra-positional omniscience, the full imaginary relation. In *American Graffiti* this contradiction of a process of production and the denial of that process takes form around the fact that we know, from the beginning of the narrative, that Curt Henderson will leave the town and yet that we hover, in suspense, over a decision which, once resolved, is obvious. The question, as always in classical realism, is one of identity. This identity may be questioned and suspended, but it is, in a deferred moment, asserted and read back over the text. Nor is this reading back an optional extra. Without it the very concept of identity and truth, the very concept of character, on which classical realism rests would disintegrate. If the hero was not really good (or bad or whatever) all along then there would be no point to the story – the narrative would become merely the retailing of successive states of affairs. The resolution of the identity of Curt Henderson is also the production for the viewer of that point of view from which he can watch the film, but the pleasure of this production is provided by two looks which threaten to disturb that point of view, to displace an identity. These looks are each of a different order and I want to consider them separately, for one remains within the order of pleasure guaranteed by the point of view while the other threatens a disruption of a very different order.

The first look that introduces the moment of heterogeneity and surplus which is the impetus of the narrative comes from the girl in the white T-bird.[3] Securely placed within a point-of-view shot (Curt Henderson's) it nevertheless troubles a full imaginary identity – throwing open an uncertainty about Curt and his future on the night he has to decide whether to leave town. It is explicitly a gaze of sexuality and introduces the unsettling evidence of woman's desire as the girl mouths 'I love you'. *American Graffiti* thus traverses the classical path of narrative in that it is a desperate attempt to deny sexuality, the knowledge of which provides its first impetus. The girl's glance introduces a look into our point of view and calls attention to our position as we become separated from our full being in the world (as Curt becomes an other for someone he does not know, so he becomes aware of his position, loses the full security of the imaginary). In order to replace ourselves fully in the world it is necessary to refind an origin which can function as a guarantee of identity. In order to overcome the unsettling gaze of the mother we must find a father, someone who will figure as that moment of originating identity and power which will deny the possibility of the inter-play of looks. It is this search that Curt Henderson undertakes. His progress from the school-teacher to the Pharaohs to Wolfman Jack is the search for a father who will confirm him in his identity and expunge the possibility of difference; who will reassert the point of view over the look. In the scene in the radio studio we have another very heavily marked point-of-view sequence (three shots of Curt watching, two of Wolfman Jack performing, in exactly the same sequence as we had earlier seen the blonde at the traffic lights) which provides the knowledge to overcome the earlier threat.

It might be objected that this approach ignores the complicated intercrossing of the stories of the four boys. But not only can one find the same logic at play in two of the other three (Milner constitutes a special case), it would also be a mistake to think they are on the same level. *Nashville* and *American Graffiti* are two of a set of films which, although they have borrowed tricks and devices from other cinemas, remain within a traditional Hollywood practice. The two most obvious tricks are the refusal to weight the sound track in the traditional manner, a development drawing on such different sources as Welles, Godard and cinéma-vérité, and, on the other hand, a proliferation of characters such that the dominance of narrative has been replaced by the freedom of the 'slice of life'. Both these novelties function as noise rather than structure. A close analysis of the sound shows that a traditional weighting is given to those elements necessary for the development of the narrative. Equally the proliferation of characters does not affect the traditional movement of narrative. Rivette's *Out One: Spectre* is an example of a film which does break down narrative by proliferation of character, but at the cost of an enormous extension of the duration of the film and a genuine inability to find it an *end*.

It is Curt Henderson's point of view which offers within the narrative that knowledge and security we enjoy as we sit in the cinema, and it is this visual primacy which indicates his traditional centrality to the narrative. For Curt accomplishes the final imaginary task – he discovers the father. For everyone else Wolfman Jack is a name which finds its reality only in the differential world of sound but Curt is able to reunite name and bearer so that a full presence can provide the certainty of what he is and what he must do – he is a *seer* and must leave town in order to see the world. The girl's gaze troubled this identity but in the final shots of the film Curt is in a position where that gaze cannot trouble him. Before she knew who and where he was – now the positions are reversed. And it is from the point of view of the plane that the film accomplishes the progress towards the knowledge implicit in it from the beginning. The primacy of Curt's progress for an understanding of the film is underlined when the final titles tell us that he is now a writer living in Canada. The implication is that it is he who has written the story, he has conferred on us his point of view.

The other look within the film is of a different order and radically displaces the point of view, introducing a far more threatening moment of separation for the spectator. This look does not occur within the diegetic space between characters but in the space between screen and audience. John Milner and Carol attack a car whose occupants have been so foolish as to throw something at them, racing round it letting down its tyres and covering it in foam. As this happens, changes of camera position are no longer motivated either by point-of-view shots or by diegetic considerations – for a moment we have lost our position and point of view as the camera breaks the 180-degree rule, though this losing of position has a certain diegetic motivation in the actions of John and Carol. Most significantly, we see the film lights appear beside the car. The diegetic space is broken up as the film looks back at us. This encounter with the real, this movement into the symbolic is the moment of ecstasy in which Carol squirts foam all over the car and Milner lets down all the tyres (a sexual symbolism obvious enough), showing us that the pleasure involved here is of a more radical nature – a pleasure of tension and its release. If Curt provides the pleasure of security and position, John Milner functions as that threatening repetition which can only end in death and which offers no position but rather ceaseless motion. This is not to suggest that Milner offers any real alternative in the film; if he did it would contaminate the pleasure provided by Curt more significantly. But as the representative of an element which finds its definition outside the synchronic space of the other characters, he introduces time in a potentially threatening way. The political nature of the film, as will be argued later, depends on a repression of time outside a process of natural growth. Milner introduces, admittedly in a minimal way, a time which is not reducible to this natural cycle – his attitude to the culture is different from that of the other boys, because he is older than they.

The question of the audience

What has been said so far may seem to have removed all questions of realism and film from any consideration of their social conditions of production and reception. Concentration on the organisation of the text has proposed a viewer caught only within an atemporal movement between the symbolic and the imaginary and confronted only by the reality of difference. It might seem from this that film and, by implication, art in general, are caught in an eternal battle between the imaginary fullness of ideology and the real emptiness of the symbolic. Nothing could be further from my intentions in this article. My aim is to introduce certain general concepts which can be used to analyse film in a determinate social moment. That the breaking of the imaginary relation between text and viewer is the first pre-requisite of political questions in art has, I would hold, been evident since Brecht. That the breaking of the imaginary relationship can constitute a political goal in itself is the ultra-leftist fantasy of the surrealists and of much of the avant-garde work now being undertaken in the cinema. In certain of their formulations this position is given a theoretical backing by the writers of the *Tel Quel* group.

I hope that my analysis of *American Graffiti* has sketched in outline how the process of the production of a point of view for the spectator is effaced by mechanisms of identification. What is politically important about this textual organisation is that it removes the spectator from the realm of contradiction. But it is not just contradiction in general that is avoided but a specific set of contradictions – those raised by the impact of the Vietnam war on American society. Portrait of a pre-Vietnam America, the film presents to us the children of the Kennedy generation in the age of innocence – an innocence that we can regard from our position of knowledge. But this knowledge presupposes us outside politics now, outside contradiction. Indeed, Curt Henderson is a writer living in Canada, reflecting on an earlier reality of America that could not be sustained. (The fact that the writer is living in Canada is a further index of the repression of Vietnam – he has presumably dodged the draft, but this remains unspoken: to interrogate that decision would introduce contradiction.) The passing of innocence is reduced in the film to the process of growing up – there is no way in which external forces could be introduced into the homogeneous society of small-town

73

California. Toad grows up and goes off to die at An Loc but this is simply part of a human cycle. The position of the viewer after the Vietnam war is simply held to be the same but different – the position of the imaginary. The Vietnam war is repressed and smoothed over.

However, if this is our criticism of the film it is clear that what we object to is not the fact that bits of reality have somehow got left out, but rather the whole relation of the film to its audience. The audience and their representations are the terms of the 'realism' of any film or work of art – not some pre-existent realtiy which it merely conveys. Nor should this be thought novel within the socialist tradition, for I would argue that Engels's and Lenin's comments on realism are prompted by these considerations, and if they used what tools they had to hand and are thus given to talking in representational terms then we, seventy years later, should not be worried about discarding these terms.

In his letter to Minna Kautsky of 26 November 1885 on her novel *The Old and the New*, Engels wrote that he had nothing against politically didactic writing, but then went on to say:

> But I believe the tendency must spring forth from the situation and the action itself, without explicit attention called to it; the writer is not obliged to offer to the readers the future historical solution of the social conflicts he depicts. Especially in our conditions, the novel primarily finds its readers in bourgeois circles, circles not directly related to our own, and there the socialist tendentious novel can fully achieve its purpose, in my view, if, by conscientiously describing the real mutual relations, it breaks down the conventional illusions dominating them, shatters the optimism of the bourgeois world, causes doubts about the validity of the existing order, and this without directly offering a solution or even, under some circumstances, taking an ostensibly partisan stand.

Within this passage Engels is using more than one criteria of realism. He calls not simply for a description of the real mutual relations but for one such that they will be directly related to their audience. The text is determined not only by the situation to be represented but by its audience as well. These considerations also dominate Lenin's writing on literature. In the articles on Tolstoy which contain his most lengthy consideration of literary matters, the present political conjuncture is always dominant. Before all else it is essential to grasp the political situation to which they are addressed. They are written to combat two prevailing views of Tolstoy – opposed but complementary. On the one hand, Lenin wishes to wrest Tolstoy from those reactionary critics who want to clasp the religious Tolstoy to their bosom and thus present him as fundamentally in favour of the status quo. On the other hand, Lenin is concerned to correct those on the left like Plekhanov who see no more in Tolstoy than a religious mystic and thus reject his work as of no value. Left and right within this circle can agree on the identity of Tolstoy. Lenin, however, protests that there is no such identity, but rather a set of contradictions which must be grasped and understood as an urgent political task. Lenin never ceases to emphasise that the reality of Tolstoy is contradictory – that it is composed both of a bitter and undying enmity for the social system which has brought about the social conditions in Russia but that this enmity goes together with the most reactionary mystical and religious ideology with the result that Tolstoy*ism* is a profound obstacle to revolutionary change in Russia. In addition to this emphasis on change and contradiction Lenin is emphatic that Tolstoy is typical, that he 'represents' the period 1861–1905, the period, that is, between the freeing of the serfs and the unsuccessful revolution of 1905. Understanding the contradiction that is Tolstoy is important because it 'represents' on the literary level the political problem of the peasantry in Russia – the peasantry is a force of great revolutionary potential and yet it is held back by a very reactionary ideology. Only by understanding these two contradictory facets can one correctly analyse the situation in Russia.

It is important to have these facts clear before considering the problem of the vocabulary Lenin uses in these articles, a vocabulary of expression and representation which finds its most characteristic form in the metaphor of the mirror. Indeed the first article on Tolstoy is entitled 'Leo Tolstoy as the mirror of the Russian Revolution' and it begins with the following paragraph:

> To identify the great artist with the revolution [of 1905] which he has obviously failed to understand, and from which he obviously stands aloof, may at first sight seem strange and artificial. A mirror which does not reflect things correctly could hardly be called a mirror. Our revolution, however, is an extremely complicated thing. Among the mass of those who are directly making and participating in it there

are many social elements which have obviously not understood what is taking place and which also stand aloof from the real historical tasks with which the course of events has confronted them. And if we have before us a really great artist, he must have reflected in his work at least some of the aspects of the revolution.

Thus this mirror that is Tolstoy and his work are so described that the metaphor cannot function coherently. Not only is it a mirror that does not reflect, it is also a mirror that participates in a process without understanding it and, as a participant, must presumably be affected by and affect that process. It is a mirror that acts. A mirror that alters the very scene it is reflecting. To complete the paragraph Lenin adds an assertion which has nothing to do with what has gone before. In any case, he argues, Tolstoy is a great artist and if this is so then his work *must* reflect his time. Thus within Lenin's text we can discern two claims. First that to understand Tolstoy is to understand the period 1861–1905 (here Tolstoy is a mirror but a mirror which acts) and second that the relation between Tolstoy and his time is the necessary relation that holds between a great artist and the society in which he lives and works.

These opening remarks provide Lenin with the space to go on to say that Tolstoy is of such supreme importance not because he represents a reactionary peasant ideology which already exists, but rather because he produces an ideology which the peasant is likely to espouse. And this production of ideology is not a separate activity from Tolstoy's writing. Ideology is produced within the work of literature; in so far as the artist is able to grasp and articulate the social changes taking place within the world of individuals and feelings, within the world of identification, he will offer an explanation of them; he will proffer an ideology. In so far as the reader is offered both a description and an explanation of his or her own life (and the description and explanation are one and the same process), he or she may adopt the ideological viewpoint of the text. It is here that ideology accomplishes its real effects, as the representation of the real conditions of existence affects those conditions themselves. Tolstoy's skill as a writer is part and contradictory parcel of his importance as a reactionary ideologue and both must be understood to understand the peasantry. For Lenin, as for Engels, what is at issue is not simply the reality external to the text but the reality of the text itself.

We must understand the text's effectivity within the social process, which is to say we have to consider the relation between reader and text in its historical specificity.

Conclusions and consequences

In my earlier article, 'Realism and the cinema: notes on some Brechtian theses' I argued for a typology of texts classified according to the organisation of discourses within them. What was crucial was not the content of the text but the relations inscribed for the reader. The real was not an external object represented in the text but the relation between text and reader which reduplicated or cut across the subject's relation to his or her experience. Classically, realism depended on obscuring the relation between text and reader in favour of a dominance accorded to a supposedly given reality, but this dominance, far from sustaining a 'natural' relation, was the product of a definite organisation which, of necessity, effaced its own workings. In so far as the 'reality' thus granted dominance was in contradiction with the ideologically dominant determinations of reality, then a text could be deemed progressive, but nevertheless such an organisation was fundamentally reactionary for it posed a reality which existed independently of both the text's and the reader's activity, a reality which was essentially non-contradictory and unchangeable. Alternatively one could have an organisation of discourses which broke with any dominance and which, as such, remained essentially subversive of any ideological order. At the end of the article I raised the question as to whether there could be a revolutionary film which would subvert the traditional position of the spectator in a more positive fashion than the simple deconstruction of the subversive film or whether any such positivity inevitably replaced one in a position of imaginary dominance.

Although I think that the earlier article can be read in a more favourable light, there is no doubt that it is contaminated by formalism; by a structuralism that it claimed to have left behind. Traditional criticism holds text and author/reader separate, with the author able to inject meaning which is then passed on to the reader. The position outlined in my article made the subject the effect of the structure (the subject is simply the sum of positions allocated to it) but it preserved the inviolability and separateness of the text — no longer given as an immutable content fixed in its determinations by reality through the author, but rather as immutable structure determining reality and author/reader in their positions. But the text has no such separate existence. If we dissolve the reader into the text in the system of identification which I have outlined in this article, it is impossible to hold text and reader (or author as first reader) separate. Rather it is a question of analysing a film within a determinate social moment so that it is possible to determine what identifications will be made and by whom, the way Lenin analyses Tolstoy. The text has no separate existence and, for this reason, it is impossible to demand a typology of texts such as I proposed in my earlier article. Rather each reading must be a specific analysis which may use certain general concepts but these concepts will find their articulation within the specific analyses and not within an already defined combinatory.

Realism is no longer a question of an exterior reality nor of the relation of reader to text, but one of the ways in which these two interact. The film-maker must draw the viewer's attention to his or her relation to the screen in order to make him or her 'realise' the social relations that are being portrayed. Inversely one could say that it is the 'strangeness' of the social relations displayed which draws the viewer's attention to the fact that he or she is watching a film. It is at the moment that an identification is broken, becomes difficult to hold, that we grasp in one and the same moment both the relations that determine that identity and our relation to its representation. Oshima's *Death by Hanging* offers an excellent example of a film in which the indissociability of 'the real' from reality is demonstrated, in which the learning of our position in the cinema is also the learning of the social reality of Japan. (It would be in terms of the way that the artist analyses our moments of constitutive separation in terms of social reality that one might formulate a justification for Lenin's unsubstantiated claim that any great artist must 'reflect' the great social changes of his time.) In *Death by Hanging*, R, having failed to die, must learn who he is so that he can be hanged again fully conscious of his crime. As he learns to take up his position sexually and socially so that he can understand why he, a Korean subproletarian, raped and murdered a Japanese girl, so we too are learning what it is to sit in the cinema. The documentary style of the opening of the film merges into fiction and then fantasy without any of the conventional markers. We have constantly to re-find our place, both in the execution hut and in the story. Subjective shots are eschewed, as are the normal rules for the organisation of cinematic space. One of the results of the lack of subjective shots is that they can be used to great effect at certain moments, as when R confronts the girl he will attack. At the narrative level we are constantly unsure both of the status of events (fact, fiction or fantasy within fiction) but also of how to understand the 'ridiculous' prison officers. As we watch the Education Officer there is a kind of irony at work which completely undercuts any position of knowledge. In a film like *American Graffiti* we can find a very classical irony whereby we are constantly aware that everything is too perfect to be true, but this irony simply confirms us in our dominance, for the perfection guarantees the imaginary truth of the story. In *Death by Hanging*, the comic antics of the Education Officer deprive us of any fixed position from which we could gather his activities into a coherent 'character'. Unable to 'place' him, we are forced to pay attention to him, to listen to his ridiculous logic, outside any certain realm of truth. The irony of *Death by Hanging* dissolves any area of truth which could be established by judging its correspondence to reality. Story of an identity (R must learn who he is), *Death by Hanging* dissolves the identity into a set of relationships which once grasped can be transformed. It is because he has understood them as a set of relationships that R can transform them at the end of the film. The introduction of his sister introduces a reality into his fantasies which means that he can no longer act them out in the real world. As this introduction of a radical otherness destroys R's fantasies so the film destroys our fantasies by the introduction of its own reality. At the end of the film we no longer have our fantasies of Koreans, of executions but only on the condition that we no longer have our fantasy of the cinema.

The cost of ignoring these considerations can be seen in the TV play *The Lump*, produced by Tony Garnett, written by Jim Allen and directed by Jack Gold in 1969. Posed once again as a problem of identity – will the young student who has taken part in the strike on the building site be won to the truth of the revolutionary cause, or will he prefer to opt out and reveal his weakness? – *The Lump* contains all its material within the most conventional diegetic and cinematic space. As a result of this imprisonment it is impossible for the film-makers to introduce any historical component – the relations of the present struggle to the Russian Revolution or to the experience of Thomas Hardy – without such forced diegetic motivation – a poster of Lenin, the example of the slogan 'Peace, Land, Bread', a bedside copy of *Jude the Obscure* – that the purpose of the reference is lost except on those who know it already. At the same time it is impossible to introduce any element of criticism or information which would not fracture the transparent space and make us aware that we are watching a 'political' film. Thus there can be no criticism of the attitude to women within the text (women are expunged completely from this world of identity except for Yorky's comment that he wants 'to get a leg over'), nor can there be any real information about the conditions of the Irish workers that cannot be 'realistically' conveyed in a short speech by a character. The introduction of any of these elements might be held to destroy the popular appeal of the film and deprive the makers of the possibility of arousing the support of a mass audience for the scandals of the building industry, and more generally for the support of left-wing views. But the content of the left-wing commitment is so vague, as a necessary consequence of the refusal to introduce the spectator to his or her own constitutive contradictions, that it is doubtful whether anybody is won by the film to anything. The mechanisms at work in *The Lump* are the same as those used in *The Sweeney* to elicit sympathy for a copper who bends the rules. One can lend this sympathy for an hour without having to change one's attitudes or beliefs because of the occultation of the relation between viewer and text which allows the spectator to remain both on and off screen in that interchange I have already sketched. It is by the interruption of that channel that one begins engagement with the real – until then there is simply the endless repetition of the imaginary.

Notes

1. A good survey of Bazin's comments on realism can be found in Christopher Williams (1973/4).
2. The particular examples used in this article were dictated by the SEFT Weekend School on realism and the cinema where the arguments were first formulated. The films planned for screening at that school were *American Graffiti*, as an example of a Hollywood film considered at the time of its

release to be in a more modern, 'realistic' style, *The Lump*, as an example of the use of fictionalised documentary for political ends, and *Death by Hanging* as an example of a film which, while superficially 'non-realist', can lay claim for inclusion within Brecht's definition of realism.

3. The analysis of the interplay of identification and vision leans heavily on articles by Stephen Heath and Laura Mulvey both published in *Screen* in 1975.

On discourse

Etymologically discourse finds its origin in the Latin verb *discurrere*, to run about, probably by way of the French form *discourir*. This particular genealogy is more indicative than it might first appear because discourse, as the term is used in classical rhetoric, emphasises language as motion, as action. If the rhetorician was concerned with arresting language so that he could specify the various relations into which words could enter, to classify the figures and the topics, discourse constituted both the object and the aim of the study. Rhetoric started from and ended with the running together of the forms and the subjects in a continuous utterance – in, exactly, a discourse. It is within this perspective that we can consider discourse as indicating the articulation of language over units greater than the sentence. The major divisions of rhetoric accomplish just such suprasentential divisions: *exordium, narratio, argumentatio, refutatio, peroratio* (Curtius 1953: 70). A particular set of articulations will produce a field of discursivity – the site of the possibility of proof and disproof (it can be recalled that the study of rhetoric found its early rationale in relation to forms of popular law (cf. Barthes 1970b: 175)). It is to such a notion of discourse that *Cahiers pour l'Analyse* made reference when, in the *avertissement* to the first number, Jacques-Alain Miller defined the magazine's task as the constitution of a theory of discourse, specifying that by discourse 'we understand a process of language that truth constrains' (1966: 5). And, in a reference to the content of that first number, Miller made clear that the constraint of truth has as its inevitable corollary the production of a subject, a subject divided by the very process of language that calls it into being.

It is this division of the subject in language, a division figured in the Lacanian concept of the signifier, which is essential to the elaboration of any theory of discourse. Without it, and whatever its lexical possibilities, the term 'discourse' no longer indicates the site(s) of the articulations of language and sociality but simply functions as a cover for a linguistic formalism or a sociological subjectivism. The linguists Zellig Harris (1952 a&b) and Emile Benveniste (1971) will serve as important examples of these alternative hazards. If the Lacanian concept of the signifier articulates the initial support for the argument, the considerations advanced will necessitate further questions, ones that will lead, by way of the consideration of the work of Michel Pêcheux, to the problem of the politics of the signifier.[1]

Emile Benveniste and the status of the subject

Benveniste's use of discourse emphasises the lexical reference to the intersubjective use of language. In his famous article on the relation of tenses in the French verb he emphasises that 'Discourse must be understood in its widest sense: every utterance assuming a speaker and a hearer, and in the speaker, the intention of influencing the other in some way.' (1971: 208–9) Such a personal use of language must be differential from the unpersonal mode of *histoire*. Benveniste uses this distinction to give an account of the tenses of the French verb. His starting-point is the apparent redundancy of forms of the past tense which change according to whether one is speaking or writing. That used in the spoken language is a compound past tense formed by the verb *avoir* (to have) and the past participle (and hereafter called the perfect), that in the written is a distinct inflection of the verb (and hereafter called the aorist). It is a commonplace amongst both native speakers and linguists that the aorist, which is the older form, is disappearing and that it will be replaced, in time, by the perfect. It is this commonplace that Benveniste is concerned to dispute. Benveniste wishes to demonstrate that, despite its long disappearance from the spoken language, there is no question that it is similarly menaced in the written language, and this because despite appearances, it serves a different function from the perfect. What is needed to determine the future of the aorist is not statistical studies but an understanding of the tense system of the French verb. The double entry for the past tense is not a redundancy which the language has been slow to remedy but the visible evidence of the fact that there are two separate tense systems which are differentiated by the relation of the speaker/writer (hereafter called *the subject of the enunciation*) to the statement (hereafter called *the enounced*). In that relation which Benveniste terms *histoire*[2] 'events that took place at a certain moment of time are presented without any intervention of the speaker in the narration' (1971: 206). The tenses of this relation are the imperfect (with which Benveniste includes the conditional), the aorist and the pluperfect together with the atemporal present of definition and a compound tense which Benveniste suggests should be called the prospective. Benveniste notes that these three basic tenses articulate perfectly the world of *histoire* and demonstrates this with quotations from a history text and a Balzac novel (examples which, as we shall see, have a great deal more significance than Benveniste would assign to them):

> There is no reason for them to change as long as the historical narration is being pursued and, furthermore, there is no reason for the narration to come to a standstill since we can imagine the whole past of the world as being a continuous narration, entirely constructed according to this triple correlation of tenses: aorist, imperfect and pluperfect. It is sufficient and necessary that the author remain faithful to his historical purpose and that he proscribe everything that is alien to the narration of events (discourse, reflections, comparisons). As a matter of fact, there is no longer even a narrator. The events are set forth chronologically, as they occurred. No one speaks here; the events seem to narrate themselves. The fundamental tense is the aorist, which is the tense of the event outside the person of a narrator. (1971: 208)

This is the impersonal relation that is opposed to *discours*. *Histoire* produces no involvement of the subject of the enunciation in the enounced while it is the very definition of *discours*. In speech the tenses are always related to the present instance and must thus give way to a tense which defines its pastness in terms of the present: 'Like the present, the perfect belongs to the linguistic system of discourse, for the temporal location of the perfect is the moment of the discourse, while the location of the aorist is the moment of the event' (1971: 210). By thus distinguishing the two forms of the past in French, Benveniste can also explain further features of the tense system. In particular, he demonstrates how the secondary compound tenses are produced in response to the pressure created around the first person forms of the two past tenses.[3]

It is not accidental that it is the first person which Benveniste isolates as the crucial articulation in the historical development of the language, for it is the category of person which provides the field within which Benveniste's tense distinctions are articulated. On the one hand there is the world of *discours*, the world of *je/tu* (I/you). On the other is the world without person, the world of *histoire*, the world of *il* (he/it). It is the emphasis on person which links this article to the others collected in Section 5 of the *Problems in General Linguistics*. The constant theme of this section is that the apparently regular structure of the three persons in many Indo-European languages is grossly misleading for the analysis of person. There are not, in fact, three persons but two *je/tu* which find themselves in opposition to a realm of 'non-person' *il*. Benveniste finds an awareness of this in the Arab grammarian's analysis of person which distinguishes the first and second person, 'he who speaks' and 'he who is spoken to' from the third 'he who is absent'. This division marks the asymmetry between the persons, an asymmetry which finds further support in the fact that in many languages the third person is unmarked in relation to the first and second and that the third person pronoun is not a universal phenomenon.

The argument so far outlined would seem to rest its analyses on a distinction between subjective and objective functions in language. Language is the combination of two autonomous but intersecting systems: the world of the first and second person, which define a subjective realm of *discours* with a tense system related to the moment of speech, and the world of the third person, which defines an objective realm of *histoire* with a tense system related to the moment of the event. It should be noted that, even granted Benveniste's assumptions, the distinction suffers from certain crucial weaknesses. Firstly there is the occurrence of the third person within the realm of *discours*, an embarrassment which provides some of Benveniste's weakest arguments: even if it is not explicit, the relationship of person is everywhere present in *discours*; it is only with *histoire* that we reach the 'true' realm of the non-person (1971:209). Secondly, and just as serious, is the fact that the anchor-tense of *discours*, the present, occurs within *histoire*; which occurrence Benveniste terms 'an atemporal present like the present of definition' (1971: 207).

Apart from such internal inconsistencies, however, there are more serious criticisms to be levelled at the whole project. Benveniste fails to give any account of the relation between the two systems which does not fall back into the subjective/ objective couple. Objective, as always on this account, becomes the paring away of the *contingent* effects of subjectivity to arrive at the necessary relations beneath. Language, with an equal familiarity, is defined as a simple mirror to reflect reality, which becomes opaque once the realm of reason is disturbed by the illogicalities of passion. This caricature is designed to highlight the similarity of this position to the traditional denigration of the order of language in relation to the speaker (rhetoric) as opposed to the order of language in relation to the facts (logic). That this caricature captures at least some of the elements of Benveniste's position is evident in sections of the article on the use of pronouns:

> If each speaker, in order to express the feeling he has of his irreducible subjectivity, made use of a distinct identifying signal (in the sense in which each radio transmitting station has its own call letters), there would be as many languages as individuals and communication would become absolutely impossible. Language wards off this danger by instituting a unique but mobile sign, I, which can be assumed by each speaker on the condition that he refers each time only to the instance of his own discourse. (1971:220)

This formulation approaches dangerously close to the Port-Royal conception of pronouns which holds that pronouns are simply used to avoid unnecessary repetition but are granted no effectivity of their own (cf. Arnauld and Lancelot 1969: 43–4), a conception which informs the whole of Port-Royal's theory of discourse. But that Benveniste's position is more ambiguous is indicated by the fact that he considers pronouns to be 'absolutely' essential to language function although he offers no theoretical justification of this absoluteness. It is when he approaches the question of subjectivity in language directly that these contradictions manifest themselves most clearly. For while the distinction *discours/ histoire* would ultimately seem to rest on a clear distinction between the subject using the language and the language, Benveniste explicitly refuses such a position in a paper written practically simultaneously:

> We are always inclined to that naive concept of a primordial period in which a complete man discovered another one, equally complete, and between the two of them language was worked out little by little. This is pure fiction. We can never get back to man separated from language and we shall never see him inventing it ... It is a speaking man whom we find in the world, a man speaking to another man, and language provides the very definition of man.   (1971: 224)

It is clear that Benveniste considers that language is constituted in relation to the other. But he fails to investigate the linguistic basis of this other, and in what amounts to a tacit acceptance of a personalist other, he is left, however reluctantly, with an account which though it interrogates its own foundations at certain moments, is finally dependent if it is to be retained in its totality, on a classic account of subjectivity. The miscognition on which Benveniste's theory rests is the failure to grasp two elements as participating in the same structure. To distinguish them as elements is his major contribution; the task that remains is to provide the structure that articulates them and such an articulation will depend on cutting back across some of the original distinctions. To oppose *je/tu* to *il* is to shatter the assumptions that make the passage from 'I' to 'you' to 'he' to 'it' an inevitable and obvious progression but to ignore their interrelation is to ignore that I/you can only function as the deictic categories for the subject of the enunciation after the passage through the third person; a passage which allows this pronoun to assume both personal and impersonal forms. Similarly *discours* is determined in its forms by *histoire* for it is the involvement of the subject of the enunciation in *histoire* that determines its appearance in the enounced of *discours*.

The interrelation is analysed in Luce Irigaray's 'Communications linguistique et spéculaire' (1966). In my summary of this argument it is important to recognise that what is in question is a diachronic fable of a synchronic functioning. In the development of the child there is a moment when the infant (*infans*: unable to speak) enters language. In this process of entry, he/she becomes aware of certain places which he/she as subject can occupy – these are the points of insertion into language. Crucially this involves the learning of pronouns: the realisation that the 'you' with which the child is addressed by the father or mother can be permutated with an 'I' in a situation from which it is excluded – when the parents speak to each other. This realisation is the understanding that the 'you' with which he or she is addressed can be permutated with a 'he' or 'she', which is the possibility that the proper name is articulated in a set of differences – and that the child is only a signifier constantly defined and redefined by a set of substitution relations. The binary I/you is transformed from two terms into a relational structure by the passage through the empty place of the 'he' or 'she' and it is through the experience of this empty place that the child enters language. The passage through this empty place is the exclusion necessary to the proper control of language and the experience of this exclusion is the first taste of annihilation – the constitutive moment at which the entry into human life is preceded by a voyage through death. It is this which gives language its fearsome quality because the experience of the sign involves a castration at the linguistic level; a castration acknowledged in medieval depictions of grammar. The crucial text for the medieval description of the liberal arts was Martianus Capella's *De nuptiis Philologiae et Mercurii* (The wedding of Philology and Mercury). Curtius gives a thorough summary: Lacking a bride, Mercury is counselled to marry the learned maid Philologia. The major part of the poem is taken up with Philologia's admittance to the rank of the Gods: 'Philologia is adorned by her mother Phronesis and greeted by the four Cardinal Virtues and the three graces. At the bidding of Athanasia, she is forced to vomit up a number of books in order to become worthy of immortality. She then ascends to heaven in a litter born by the youths Labor and Amor and the maidens Epimelia (application) and Agrypnia (the intellectual worker's night labours and curtailed sleep).' More crucial for a metaphorical understanding of the process I have just traced is the appearance of Grammar: 'Grammar appears as a gray-haired woman of advanced age, who boasts that she descends from the Egyptian king Osiris. Later she lived for a long time in Attica, but now she appears in Roman dress. She carries an ebony casket, containing a knife and a file with which to operate surgically on childrens' grammatical errors' (Curtius 1953:38–9).

To accede to the world of absence – to the world of the sign where one thing can stand for another – we must wound perpetually, if not destroy, a narcissism which would render the world dependent on our presence. This process is also the engenderment of the 'one' of identity in a contradictory movement by which this absence is taken up and named; this naming thus conferring a unity and an identity, a presence. The proper name is transformed from a set of physical qualities into the enumerable mark of an absence. The name is that which marks the exclusion of the subject from the realm in which he/she is thus constituted. And this exclusion is constantly relived in the progress through language. When the substitution rules have been mastered, the child finds itself divided between two worlds – the world of the enunciation, where he or she is constantly in play as signifier and the world of the enounced, where he or she is constantly in place as signified.

Benveniste's great contribution is to have distinguished two different axes of language, the enunciation and the enounced, but his exposition of their relation is vitiated by his uncritical acceptance of the notion of the subject. The consequence of this acceptance is that the relationship between the subject of the enunciation and the subject of the enounced remains obscure. *Histoire* and *discours* are distinguished by the presence of the subject of the enunciation in *discours* and its absence from *histoire*. But the considerations just advanced demonstrate:

1. that the subject of the enunciation does occur in the realm of the third person because even if there is no direct appearance in the pronouns of the enounced the subject is constituted in the signifier, and thus

2. that *discours* is dependent on *histoire*, most evidently in that the predicates that can be attached to proper names will determine the place of pronouns in *discours*.

The interrelation between *discours* and *histoire* and the crucial role of proper names in this interrelation is evident in what I have termed elsewhere the classic realist text (above and MacCabe 1979). It is through the determination of the possibilities of predication that the novelist can produce the moral judgements of *discours*. What can and cannot be said in *discours* is determined by the articulations of *histoire*. A consideration

89

of Benveniste's example from Balzac will enable us to understand this functioning:

> Après un tour de galerie, le jeune homme *regarda* tour à tour le ciel et sa montre, *fit* un geste d'impatience, *entra* dans un bureau de tabac, y *alluma* un cigare, se *posa* devant une glace, et *jeta* un regard sur son costume, un peu plus riche que ne le permettent en France les lois du goût (I). Il *rajusta* son col et son gilet de velours noir sur lequel *se croisait* plusieurs fois une de ces grosses chaînes d'or fabriquées à Gênes; puis, après avoir jeté par un seul mouvement sur son épaule gauche son manteau doublé de velours en le drapant avec élégance, il *reprit* sa promenade sans se laisser distraire par les œillades bourgeoises qu'il *recevait*. Quand les boutiques *commencèrent* à s'illuminer et que la nuit lui *parut* assez noire, il *se dirigea* vers la place du Palais-Royal en homme qui *craignait* d'être reconnu, car il *côtoya* la place jusqu'à la fontaine, pour gagner à l'abri des fiacres l'entrée de la rue Froidmanteau.   (1971: 208)

When the young man had gone round the gallery, he looked up at the sky and then at his watch, made an impatient gesture, went into a tobacconist and once inside lit up a cigar. He stood in front of a mirror and glanced at his clothes which were rather more dressy than is allowed by good taste in France. (I) He straightened his collar and his black velvet waistcoat on which one of those heavy gold chains made in Genoa was crossed and recrossed several times; then after throwing over his shoulder in one smooth movement his double cloak of velvet so that it draped him in elegant folds, he resumed his walk without allowing himself to be distracted by the stares of the bourgeoisie that were directed towards him. When the shops began to light up and the evening had become dark, he made his way towards the square of Palais Royal like a man who was frightened of being recognised for he hugged the walls of the square up to the fountain so that he could reach the entry to the rue Froidmanteau under cover of the carriages.

Benveniste underlines all the occurrences of the tenses of *histoire* and for the one occurrence of a present tense he adds as a footnote (I) 'Réflexion de l'auteur qui échappe au plan du récit' (Reflection of the author which falls outside the scope of the narrative).

The crucial moment in this passage is the moment which Benveniste recognises as escaping his division, the moment at which Balzac intervenes in order to inform us that the young man's clothes are a little too overdone. Benveniste argues that this present tense relates directly to the author independently of the narrative. But this is to ignore the extent to which the figure of the author is a function of the narrative. The introduction of a present tense locates the author as omniscient in the present but his position does not find its authority in the present tense nor in the historical figure Honoré de Balzac but rather in the wealth of detailed aorists which guarantee the truth of the narrative and, by metonymy, of its writer. The relation between the tenses in this type of novel, or better this practice of writing, is not one of separation or division but of solidarity. If the aorist becomes excluded from speech, this absence becomes the guarantee of the truth of the written form. And it is this truth which justifies the present tenses that occur within a novel.[4] Benveniste's distinction between the tenses finds its basis not in some grammatical features of the verb but in a certain practice of writing which has pulled in its wake certain grammatical features.[5] A practice is defined as a transformation of material through time and a practice of writing is a constant transformation, work on the signifying material of language. It is within this perspective that one might venture certain historical explanations of the tense system in French. In particular one might be able to situate the aorist's exclusion from speech and the rise of the novel as contemporary events. As to the contemporary situation: although Benveniste provides a perfectly satisfactory synchronic account of a stable system, it does not follow that the aorist is not menaced by extinction. If Benveniste is quite right to criticise the received notion that the aorist is succumbing to some inexorable natural process, it is important to recognise that in the last forty years (and particularly in the last ten) there have arisen various practices of writing which aim at the disruption of the stable system that Benveniste describes. In his first novel *L'Etranger* Albert Camus wrote a narrative which systematically avoided the aorist and in the wake of Camus's book a variety of anti-aorist ideologies have been articulated. The refusal to use the aorist has been theorised in terms of existential authenticity (it is the tense that burdens you with a past that exhausts your definition) or of a more structural sensibility (it is the tense of the novel in which one refuses to be written) or of a political refusal of the social and educational divisions inscribed within the French language (the aorist is an 'élitist' tense). *Histoire* and *discours* depend on a distinction between a language use from which the speaking subject is excluded and a language use in which the subject can identify his/her place. The detour through psychoanalysis demonstrates that the identifying of the place by the subject is the experience of exclusion and its modalities. We cannot find a language independent of subjectivity, nor a subjectivity independent of language but must attempt to understand their joint constitution. Benveniste's analysis is a vital and important step in the attempt to understand the linguistic mechanisms across which the 'I' and the 'it' form and re-form: the process by which a subjectivity is produced, along with its constant subversion. But if Benveniste's distinction is of such crucial importance, it is necessary to recognise that because his own attempts to develop it are caught within the terms of classical philosophy, he is often forced to return, against his explicit theses, to a conception of language as transparent mirror between subject and object, a mere reflection for worlds constituted outside its operations.

Zellig Harris and the constitution of the corpus

It is now so evident that for linguistics to constitute itself as a science it was necessary to drop normative concerns that one can all too hastily recuperate such a decision within a spontaneous 'objectivist' theory of science and ignore the complex play of theories and practices that were re-aligned by the Saussurean revolution. If, until then, the grammarian had been concerned with laying down the rules and means of expression in reference to an optimum then inevitably his concern was with *texts* of considerable length in which this optimum could be demonstrated with reference to specific effectivities. Once, however, the notion of *langue* as system has been introduced, language is studied in terms of the operations which allow the possibility of the specific production of sense and *no longer* in terms of a sense which it is language's function to produce. At this point the text ceases to be an object for the linguist because the set of systems which allow combination and regular substitution are smaller than the text. Over and above the sentence we leave the domain of *langue* to enter into the world of a full subjectivity where *langue* is simply at the service of *parole*. Jakobson, in a famous passage, states the position thus:

There is an ascending scale of liberty in the combination of linguistic units. In the combination of distinctive traits into phonemes the user's liberty is nil; the code has already established all the possibilities that can be used in the language in question. In the combination of phonemes into words his liberty is heavily circumscribed; it is limited to the marginal situation of the creation of new words. The constraints upon the speaker are less when it comes to the combination of words into sentences. But finally in the combination of sentences into statements the action of the constraining rules of syntax stops and the liberty of each speaker grows substantially, although one should still not underestimate the number of stereotyped statements. (Jakobson 1963: 47)

This belief in the creative freedom of the individual at the supra-sentential level (freedom limited only by what guarantees its reality – the risk of stereotype) has effectively vitiated the majority of work done by linguists on discourse analysis, or, as it is also described, text-linguistics.[6] If the lexical ambiguity of the term discourse indicates that the articulatory and intersubjective functions of language are *one and the same*, that it is the major articulations of language which provide the field for the appearance of subjectivity, the example of Benveniste proves that as long as the problem of the subject is left unresolved then the analysis will collapse back into the presuppositions of the Saussurean concept of *parole*. To analyse discourse we must start from Lacan's insight that language operates on a continuous misconstruction of its constitution; which misconstruction is the appearance of the subject.

In this perspective the work of Zellig Harris provides a much more promising start in its resolute refusal of any problematic of subjectivity although we shall also see how this refusal blocks Harris's own development of his procedures of analysis. For Harris the failure of linguistics to pass beyond the threshold of the sentence can be ascribed to the fact that effective grammars can be constituted without so doing. In his concern to propose an analysis which does move beyond the sentence, Harris's starting-point is a definition of discourse as 'connected speech or writing', a definition which starts from the very opposite emphasis to Benveniste's intersubjectivity. Harris believes that there are regularities and constraints to be discovered at the level of discourse and, further, that these discoveries will relate language to its cultural situation: to the problem of subjectivity. However, the problem of subjectivity is left to a further stage of the analysis which must start from the formal investigation of particular texts. The choice of particular texts as the corpus is determined for Harris by two considerations. First, we can discover no general supra-sentential rules because of the heterogeneity of language-use, it is only within individual texts that we can discern regularities. Second, in relation to the problem of subjectivity and language, Harris holds that the relation of discourse to its cultural situation must be investigated in individual instances because the relation *changes in each instance*. Thus discourse analysis, by concentrating on one continuous text, allows both the construction of regularities that go beyond the sentence and, at the same time, the possibility of studying the relations between these regularities and the conditions of the production of the text. The method pre-supposes no knowledge except that of morpheme boundaries but, in fact, Harris uses grammatical knowledge in order to construct larger equivalence classes, a concept we shall come to in a moment. Harris summarises his position at the end of the introduction to the article 'Discourse analysis' thus: 'We have raised two problems: that of distributional relations among sentences, and that of the correlation between language and social situation. We have proposed that information relevant to both of these problems can be obtained by a formal analysis of one stretch of discourse at a time' (Harris 1952 a: 4–5). We shall return to these arguments after considering Harris's procedures.

The distributional methods that Harris proposes for the analysis of discourse are derived from those set out in Harris's *Methods in Structural Linguistics* which had been published the year before although composed some time earlier (it has since been reissued as *Structural Linguistics*). Lyons describes the methodology as follows:

> it was assumed that the proper task of 'structural linguistics' was to formulate a technique, or procedure, which could be applied to a corpus of attested utterances and, with the minimum use of the informant's judgements of 'sameness' and 'difference', could be guaranteed to derive the rules of the grammar from the corpus itself. (1968: 157)

Starting, that is, from a *corpus*, the result of the collection of statements produced by members of the same speech community at the same time, the distributional analyst, rejecting all explanations in terms of function or meaning, attempts to subdivide the corpus in terms of contexts or *environments*. To describe an environment is to describe what precedes and follows a particular unit. The problem then becomes one of ordering the occurrences of units within similar environments with the aim of producing an account of the distribution of a unit. If we imagine a language close to English but in which, for simplicity's sake, the adjective always preceded the noun and never appeared without the noun, a distributional grammar would describe it simply as a unit A which always precedes another unit N, this second unit having the possibility of appearing without unit A and in combination with other units. This is exactly the method that Harris follows, with the proviso that the corpus is constituted by one text because of the necessity of avoiding any criteria from outside language (including meaning) in specifying the corpus.

Given the simple aim of constituting classes with the same environment and considering their appearance within a specific text so that certain patterns and regularities can be analysed, Harris's paper on structural linguistics is devoted to sketching the difficulties involved in the analysis. Taken strictly the methods of distributionalism would prevent the analysis of any but the most simple kind of text because there are just not that many identical repetitions in any normal use of language. Harris is concerned to specify criteria of equivalence which are not dependent on meaning. The construction of equivalences is a question of paraphrasing the original phrase until the element under investigation can be isolated in the same position as the one with which an equivalence is to be established. This may seem rather a circular procedure. Harris comments:

> The criterion is not some external consideration like getting the longest possible chain, but rather the intrinsic consideration of finding some patterned distribution of these classes. In other words we try to set up such classes as will have an interesting distribution in our particular text. This may seem a rather circular safeguard for constructing equivalence chains. But it simply means that whenever we have to decide whether to carry an equivalence chain one step further, we exercise the foresight of considering how the new interval will

> fit into our analysed text as it appears when represented in terms of
> the new class. This kind of consideration occurs in descriptive
> linguistics when we have to decide, for example, how far to subdivide
> a phonemic sequence into morphemes.   (Harris, 1952 a: 12)

In rearranging the position of phrases we take the horizontal order
of the segments of the sentence as immaterial. Our aim, however,
is to construct a vertical order which will reveal in the regular
distribution of the equivalence classes certain systematicities in
discourse which were not evidently available.

In determining the equivalence classes it is the division of the
sentences into segments that is crucial for 'we want not simply
the same distributional classes but the same relationship between
these classes'. Grammatical criteria will normally provide the
necessary divisions but certain cases remain problematic. Harris's
example of such a difficulty is the sentence 'Casals who is self-
exiled from Spain stopped performing after the Fascist victory.'
The problem for Harris is whether 'who' continues or repeats
Casals: 'If *who* continues *Casals*, we have one interval, the first
section (C) being *Casals who*, while the second section (S) is *self-
exiled ... stopped ...* If *who* repeats Casals instead of continuing
it, we have two intervals, one embedded in the other: the first
consists of *Casals* (again C) plus *stopped performing* (marked
S_1), the second of *who* (taken as an equivalent of Casals) plus *is
self-exiled* (S_2).' For Harris the choice simply depends on
whether we can find elements of the second half of the sentence
occuring separately. And this matter is considered relatively
unimportant by Harris: 'The only difference between taking a
dependent element as a continuation and taking it as a repetition
is the number of intervals one or two into which one can analyse
the total' (Harris 1952 a: 16–17).

Harris's comments ignore the importance of the choice of
analysis. In order to analyse the regularities of occurrence we
must know what can count as an equivalence class, for a predi-
cate which contains two verbs might not be equivalent to a predi-
cate with one. Indeed in this particular case we are dealing with
a sentence for which it is extremely unlikely that one can set up
any equivalence classes given Harris's original definition of the
corpus. For in this passage Harris glides over the problem of
relatives; a problem which is crucial to an understanding of

discourse. Traditionally relatives are analysed into restrictive and non-restrictive. The restrictive relative cannot be removed from the sentence in which it occurs without a change in meaning because it determines one of the terms within the main clause. Transformational grammars tend to analyse restrictive relatives in terms of an embedded structure whereby the relative clause is found as a sentence attached to a noun phrase in the deep structure (cf. Huddleston 1976: 101–9). Thus an analysis of the sentence 'Mary believed the rumour that John had started' produces the sentence 'John started the rumour' as dependent on 'the rumour' in the deep structure. On the other hand, the non-restrictive relative can, in principle, be abstracted from the sentence without a consequent change in meaning; thus 'Moses, who was a prophet, led the Jews out of Egypt'. Here the relative does not identify a constituent part of the main sentence. Traditionally generative grammars analyse such sentences in terms of co-ordination instead of subordination with two separate sentences in the deep structure. But this grammatical distinction is not at all clear if we consider the discursive functioning of the relative. For in the sentence 'Casals, who is self-exiled from Spain, stopped performing after the Fascist victory' *who is self-exiled* does not identify the subject of the sentence because a proper name cannot be further identified. A proper name is precisely an identification and nothing more, the enumerable mark of a specific absence. But if we consider the sentence about Casals, we can recognise that the main and subordinate clause enter into a relation which produces something over and above their separate assertions. What is asserted is a relation of consequence which escapes our grammatical analysis. Casals's exile and his refusal to perform are bound together.

In fact it is relatives which provide a key fulcrum in the functioning of discourses and this precisely because relatives produce some of the crucial subjective effects of the discourse, effects which Harris's examples demonstrate clearly although Harris never explicitly concerns himself with them.[7] In brief, and following the arguments advanced by Michel Pêcheux in *Les Vérités de la Palice* (1975), we can describe the non-restrictive relative in terms of a discourse turning back on itself and constantly providing a series of equivalences for the terms it is using. The non-restrictive relative produces evidence of an alternative

97

which would say the same thing only differently and it is this possibility of an alternative, of a set of alternatives, which constitutes the effect of sense and subjectivity and their necessary certainty. Sense does not arrive with each word but is produced across a set of alternatives within a discourse. It is this possibility which produces the effect that 'I' am in control of my discourses, that I say what I *say* because I can always go back and offer a set of explanatory alternatives: Moses – a prophet – the leader of the Jews out of Egypt, etc.

The restrictive relative, on the other hand, is the site of two discourses intersecting and being homogenised by the action of the relative. If we examine the example that Harris uses we can see that the operation in question is a binding together of the discourses of politics and music around the name of Casals. It is this 'binding' that the traditional analysis of proper names and relatives obscures by considering that the relation between Casals and the relative is one of non-restriction and, therefore, of simple co-ordination. For the elements of the sentence are held together because of the implied consequence between exile and the refusal to perform, a consequence which supports a conditional of the form 'If one is a musician (if one is Casals) then one would exile oneself from Spain and stop performing.' The proof that this relation of implication is contained in the indicative is that if one refuses the conditional then one is inclined to contest the indicative sentence. The text produces a complicity with its reader which provides the mechanism for understanding the movement from *histoire* to *discours* (in Benveniste's terms) that I have already discussed. Around the proper name is produced a general statement which then permits of substitution with 'you' or 'I'. Indeed if we think of the refusal of complicity it is obvious what is at stake. 'He doesn't care about Spain' 'He's just trying to make more money' 'He's just an artist.' Another discourse rescues us from an identification we reject.

Harris would object violently to the argument that I have just sketched. For I have assumed that I can specify discourses independently of the analysis. But we touch here at the arguments about the constitution of the corpus. By limiting himself to a single text, Harris cannot proceed very far with his explicit aim of relating the supra-sentential regularities to the cultural situation. It is extremely doubtful that the selection of the single text as a corpus can be given any justification other than there is no obvious alternative which would constitute the corpus independently of considerations of meaning. But to take this position is to ignore the reality of social institutions, however analysed, and to so ignore institutions is to run the risk of re-introducing meaning back into the field of linguistics (under the form of some logicist universal semantics). De Saussure's inauguration of linguistics takes the form of a double separation. On the one hand he separates *langue* from any problem of subjectivity (this subjectivity is not interrogated but simply re-placed in the realm of *parole*). On the other hand he separates *langue* from any other social institution because of the determinate and evident relation between means and ends in all social institutions except *langue* (cf. de Saussure 1972: 110; 1974: 76).

The error about institutions is the reverse side of the mistake which constitutes *parole* as the realm of a pure subjectivity in control of language. To presume that means are directly related to ends in institutions and find their base in some 'nature' is a naivety which is no longer tenable sixty years after de Saussure's death. Both Marxist and sociological analyses refuse such transparency to the other institutions. The functioning of an institution is not reducible to its ends and its ends are not so easily specifiable as de Saussure seems to have imagined. One of the most important of 'means' within any institution is language and if we concede that the operations of language cannot be reduced to the institutions' ends, explicit or otherwise, then it is possible to see how one can specify a discourse institutionally while still being unable to answer any of the questions about the specific functioning and effectivity of that discourse. It is this functioning and effectivity which Harris's method of analysis offers the possibility of investigating. Obviously the discursive structure thus analysed will feed back into the original social analysis in certain ways. What the discursive analysis should reveal are the different linguistic methods of identification within a specific discourse. That is to say where it can turn back on itself and propose alternatives (the working of the conscious in retrieving material from the preconscious) and there where constitutive moments of fusion do not allow of investigation without the breaking of that very identity (the unconscious of the discourse).

The arguments of this section are taken directly from, or are

Theoretical essays

simple elaborations of, the work of the French philosopher and linguist Michel Pêcheux (1969, 1975).[8] Pêcheux has argued consistently that linguistics constitutes itself by separating itself from any notion of 'subject' or 'institution' and that the refusal to theorise these notions at the level of language entails a return of the subject which haunts linguistics in the form of a universal semantics. He argues further that the only way to remove semantics as a threat to linguistics is to give an account of the effectivity of discourse which will be concerned to demonstrate how specific discursive processes work on a linguistic base to produce specific discursive effects. Discursive formations can be specified in terms of a social and ideological analysis but this specification will not demonstrate their modes of functioning. These modes of functioning may, in turn, reveal weaknesses in the original specification (Pêcheux 1978). Harris's method provides the first step towards the possibility of analysing the specific discursive processes but without a theory of ideology he cannot specify a corpus. And further, and this constitutes the second major argument against the original method, he is blind to the problem of determining those new sequences which can be generated within a discourse and those which cannot.[9]

Michel Pêcheux and the politics of the signifier

The argument of the paper so far has been as follows. If one examines Benveniste's distinction between *discours* and *histoire*, one discovers that, despite the appearance of a basis in grammar and particularly in the tenses of the French verb, this distinction rests on an unexamined notion of the subject which transforms a specific set of linguistic practices (largely practices of writing) into a set of eternal relations between subject and language which reproduce the rhetoric/logic distinction traditional to Western thought since the seventeenth century. However, in the course of his investigation Benveniste distinguished two different relations to language – the subject of the enunciation and the subject of the enounced – which are indeed central to an understanding of the functioning of language. Benveniste thought that one could specify language uses in which the subject of the enunciation was not involved (this indeed is the very definition of *histoire*) but a reflection on the psychoanalytic account of the subject contradicted this position. The crucial nexus in the

100

acquisition of language (an acquisition which, on this account, must be understood as constant, as interminable) is the moment at which the child grasps the systematic substitutability of pronouns. This moment introduces, to use Lacan's terminology, the big Other, an introduction understood *not* as the encounter with the parents on the level of demand but as the encounter with the parent as the site of language and desire which outruns any particular statement of demand. This encounter turns on the parents' speech with each other about the child. It is this experience of articulation which produces the divided subject of psychoanalysis, for on the one hand the speaker is caught up in the play of signifiers, of the differential oppositions which produce meaning independently of the activity of the individual, and, on the other, the child takes its place as the 'I' of experience and language, the unified subject of classical philosophy and modern linguistics. (The field and modalities of this division can be understood as congruent with the division which locates the child both in the movement along the play of the parents' desire, a multiplicity of positions, and in its appropriate place, its signified sexuality.)

Before proceeding further, it might be useful to consider, if only to reject, an argument to the effect that this account is merely another version of the genesis of the subject and, like all such accounts, it presupposes what it proves, having need of a subject already in place who then recognises him/her self as subject. For, the argument continues, in order to ensure recognition there must already be a subject ready to recognise its own essence but, if this is so, it implies that this essence must be autonomous of its appearance in language. A feature of man (viz. the unconscious) is made the determining principle of language. The reply to this is that the recognition in question is not the recognition of an essence but rather the recognition of the possibility of another signifier. As such it is not a question of defining man with an unconscious and then discussing language but rather a question of defining language in such a way that there is unconsiousness for he or she who wishes to speak.

It is the recognition of the division of the subject in language that enables one to pass beyond the rhetoric/logic distinction to discover the speaker at play in every function of language. Harris's article offers a technique for attempting to grasp in more detail the relation between enunciation and enounced but if it has the immense merit of refusing the classical conception of the subject, it fails completely to render a more adequate account of the subject. This weakness affects Harris's analysis at the level of the constitution of the corpus where deprived of any theory of ideology or institutions, a banal empiricism ensures no real investigation of the 'correlation between language and social situation'. Pêcheux's work over the last ten years marks the most serious attempt to develop Harris's techniques in line with a theory of discourse which attempts to take account not only of the divided subject of psychoanalysis but also of language's place within the class struggle, where language is not only the instrument of communication, so beloved of linguistic theorists, but also the instrument of non-communication, so necessary to the divisions of modern capital. Pêcheux's work is itself marked, however, by a resurgence of the rhetoric/logic model, a resurgence which corresponds to an unresolved political difficulty with Lacanian theory. In this final section I want to sketch the arguments that Pêcheux develops in *Les Vérités de la Palice* and to indicate their weaknesses.[10]

Pêcheux's starting-point is the feebleness of those Marxist positions which, garnishing themselves with one or two comments from *The German Ideology*, accept unreservedly the whole structure of communications theory complete with autonomous senders and receivers using codes to convey messages. Pêcheux, on the other hand, stresses that language functions both as communication and non-communication, that when one moves from morphology and syntax to meaning, one must leave behind the notion of *langue*, to which each speaker bears a similar relation, and consider discursive formations, specific areas of communicability that set in place both sender and receiver and which determine the appropriateness of messages. Centrally Pêcheux is concerned to establish the moments at which a scientific theory of the social formation, namely Marxism, is intimately concerned with the discursive functioning of language and he proceeds about this task by a long discussion of the analyses of relative clauses since the time of Port-Royal, a discussion that ends, as we have seen above, with a demonstration that the distinctions between relative clauses can only be understood in terms of discursive rather than grammatical function.

Port-Royal's analysis of sentences starts from the premise that one can understand the functioning of language, its grammar, in terms of the operations of the mind, operations which essentially consist of but one: predication. This position subordinates the order of grammar and rhetoric to the order of thought (a refurbished Aristotelian logic) and enables Arnauld and Lancelot to make a precise distinction between relatives in terms of the determination of the subject of the main clause. If the subject is determined by the relative then the relative simply functions as an aid in the identification of the subject and as such it can be understood as part of a rhetoric which, for Port-Royal, is now wholly defined in terms of a pedagogy. If, on the other hand, the subject can be identified independently (if it is a proper name for example) then the relative clause represents an autonomous act of judgement which must be understood in terms of the general logic of judgement.

Within Port-Royal's terms there is no problem of the subject of the enunciation. The world and its representation exist independently of the enunciation of language and thus, for example, pronouns can be explained on the grounds of economy and politeness (it would be rude to endlessly repeat one's own name – the pronoun 'I' thus saves one social embarrassment). But by the time we reach Leibniz and the British empiricists in the next century the relation between world and representation becomes less certain and the problem of the subject's place as the movement between the two becomes dominant. Leibniz solves this problem by creating an infinity of possible worlds in which the seeming alternatives offered by language find resolution if one occupies the position of God. Significantly Leibniz's position leads him to analyse all relative clauses attached to names as restrictive. The effect of this is to multiply the population considerably as there are as many persons as there are names followed by relative clauses. The John Smith in 'John Smith who left his house this morning ...' becomes different from the John Smith in 'John Smith who ate lunch in McDonald's at one o'clock ...' To understand this multiplicity of possible worlds in which representation is once again transparent we would have to be God. If Leibniz solves the problem by expanding reality to occupy the space allocated to it by language, the British empiricists undertake to reduce reality to the perspective of the subject. It is the subject who becomes the source of a language charged with no more than representing his needs or sense impressions. Thus instead of finding ourselves in a world of Leibnizian necessity, if only we were God, we occupy a world in which everything is merely a useful fiction or construction. What we can see at work in the consideration of Leibniz and the British empiricists is a movement from the problem of necessary and contingent towards the problem of subjective and objective, a problem which haunts philosophies of language up to the present day. What Pêcheux is concerned to demonstrate across a series of historical readings is that the traditional philosophical questions about language are produced within epistemological problematics and that both the rationalist and empiricist versions of language take their starting-point in a refusal to understanding the historical development of science as a set of theoretical struggles which have definite conditions of existence. Pêcheux's thesis is that the link between philosophy of language and epistemology is crucial and that as long as one does not have an adequate account of the development of science one will be stuck with a philosophy of language which will endlessly reproduce the idealist categories of subject and object instead of addressing itself to the problem of discourse and discursive formations. For Pêcheux this constitutive misunderstanding of science can essentially be resumed under two headings: those of metaphysical realism and logical empiricism:

> empiricist theories of knowledge, just as much as realist theories, seem to have a stake in forgetting the existence of historically constituted scientific disciplines to the profit of a universal theory of ideas, whether this takes the realist form of an a priori and universal network of notions or the empiricist form of an administrative procedure applicable to the universe considered as a collection of facts, objects, events or acts.   (Pêcheux 1975: 68, author's emphasis)

For Pêcheux the exemplary modern discussion of the problem of language in relation to science is Frege's and, in particular, the criticisms that Frege addressed to Husserl over the status of arithmetic. For Husserl the subject is the source and unifying principle of representations whereas for Frege the subject is the bearer of representations which it neither creates nor unifies. But if Frege succeeds in displacing the subject in his discussion of science, he fails, on the other hand, to understand the necessity of theorising the production of the subject in language. In the place of such a theory we find the dream of the production of a language from which all 'imperfections' have been removed, a dream to which one can have no objection in so far as it embodies a wish to liberate mathematics from the effects of language but which does, however, fall back into traditional concerns, if it is interpreted as the wish to liberate language from its own imperfections.[11] Once again the functioning of the relative provides a focal point for philosophical debate. Frege was worried by sentences like 'He who discovered the elliptical orbit of the planets died in poverty'. The problem for Frege is that one cannot logically disentangle the main and subordinate clauses because the main clause depends for its truth or falsity on the fact that the subordinate clause has a reference. For Frege the functioning of language produces an illusion: a pre-supposed statement of existence. What, for Frege, is a regrettable imperfection of the language is, for Pêcheux, the evidence of the functioning of language as discourse. Indeed such sentences provide the quintessential example whereby discourse produces within one domain of thought another domain of thought *as if* this other domain had already been introduced. In discourse there is no beginning for the subject who always already finds itself and its discourses in place. It is this particular functioning of the relative that Pêcheux uses as a justification for the thesis advanced by Althusser in his essay on Ideological State Apparatuses (1971) that the subject is always already interpellated in ideology. For Pêcheux it is the fact that the complex whole of the discursive formations, which he terms the *interdiscourse*, constantly provides already available positions, which he terms the *preconstructed*, within any specific discursive formation that provides the material basis for Althusser's theory of interpellation. It follows from this that the interdiscourse is identified wtih the Subject (with a big S) which Althusser had used in a reformulation (whose problems we shall shortly investigate) of Lacan's big Other. Pêcheux makes clear this equation between Subject and Other, identified materially with the interdiscourse, and attempts to distinguish this effect of the introduction of the preconstructed from another discursive function of the relative, which he terms the *support effect*, in which the relative signals a discourse turning back on itself (as in the example of Moses) rather than the introduction of the interdiscourse. This discursive function, as we saw above, is identified with the pre-concious. So, on the one hand, we can identify the support effect, the doubling back, as the construction of the effects of sense and certainty; construction along and across the possible paraphrases that constitute a discourse. It is in these alternatives (often purely grammatical) that one can locate the effect of sense and an imaginarily full subjectivity – constituted by the very possibility of doubling back and restating. In the operations of the preconstructed, on the other hand, such paraphrase is not possible because so to do would be to step outside the discourse and locate its unconscious constitution.

If this account might seem to provide an account of the division of the subject in language and relate it to the problems of ideololgical analysis and struggle, it must be recognised that the division here proposed has little to do with Lacan's concept of the subject but rather involves the construction of an ego completely dominated by a super ego. An investigation of the problems of the Althusser-Pêcheux conception will, however, enable us to pose the political problem of Lacan's concept of the signifier and the divided subject which there finds its constitution. At a simple level one could accuse Pêcheux of failing to grasp the force of the Freudian unconscious, a failure which has its effects in the description of both discursive functions. If we consider the support effect, where paraphrastic relations produce both subject and sense, we can note that even if the subject is produced as effect rather than invoked as cause, it is a subject in full control of language. But the situation of paraphrase in which Pêcheux locates both subject and sense bears witness in itself to the functioning of a desire which is absent from Pêcheux's formulations. For the request for a remark to be paraphrased is always more than a demand for clarification which allows the production of inter-subjective sense, it always entails the desire for knowledge of the other which disrupts the sense by drawing attention to the surplus of signifiers. Even in the realm of the support effect, a parapraxis can bear witness to the divided nature of the subject. Pêcheux's production of the subject in relation to sense without any possibility that the truth of language can explode on to the scene of subjectivity finds its complement in an account of the production of the unconscious which, following Althusser, provides it with all the imaginary power of an omnipotent super ego. If we recall the central scenario of Althusser's essay, it describes the action of a policeman who calls out 'hey you!', a shout to which our inevitable response is an index of the fact that we are always already there in the position of 'you', that we are always interpellated in ideology. If we compare this scenario to that sketched by Irigaray – the child listening to the parents talk about it – we can notice that Irigaray's account emphasises that the child is only present as signifier in the parents' speech in so far as it is excluded from that very speech (conscious and un-conscious are produced in the same turn of phrase). Althusser's account, from which nothing is excluded, leaves nothing un-conscious: the subject is reduced by the terrorised presence of the ego to an imaginary super ego. (Houdebine makes this point in telling fashion when he insists that the Althusserian drama should be told from the point of view of the policeman. With this difference: as the interpellated subject turns the policeman sees that he has hailed the wrong person and thus experiences, even from the position of authority, the dominance of the signifier (Houdebine 1976: 91).)[12]

To content oneself, like Houdebine, with a superior condem-nation of Althusser's ignorance of Lacan – he hasn't read the *Ecrits* properly – misses the importance of a mistake which requires, exactly, analysis. Althusser's re-articulation of Lacan is political and it comprises both a positive and negative aspect, aspects which are necessarily linked. Negatively, the identifi-cation of the Other and the Subject represses the Other as the heterogenous site of language and desire. Instead of Lacan's insistence on the impossibility of a consciousness transparent to itself, Althusser produces an omnipotent subject who is master of both language and desire. The consequence of this mastery is that there is no *theoretical* perspective for ideological struggle in the face of dominant ideologies for there is nothing which escapes or is left over from the original production of the subject by the Subject (this political pessimism coincides with the functional-ism of the concept of the Ideological State Apparatus). If Althusser had simply transported Lacan's concept of the Other into the analysis of the social formation then it would have been possible for him to give an account of the construction of subversive ideologies. A Marxist reading of the division of the subject in the place of the Other would theorise the individual's assumption of the place produced for him or her by the complex of discursive formations and would insist that these places would be constantly threatened and undermined by their constitutive instability in the field of language and desire. Such a reading of Lacan's Other would immediately, and in its very account of dominant ideologies, offer a material basis for the constuction of subversive ideologies. But, and here we come to the positive aspect of Althusser's transposition, such a Marxist reformulation of Lacan, deprived of its articulation within the drama of the Oedipus, would leave the formation of subversive ideologies, and discourses to the chance play of the signifier. Althusser's positioning of the drama of the subject in the policeman's call for identity can be read as an effort to call in question the Lacanian concept of the signifier in so far as Lacan deduces the divided subject from the very fact of language itself and makes the actual sites of language use (the family, the school, the workplace) merely unimportant variations with no effectivity inscribed in the theory (this difficulty appears within Lacanian theory itself in the status to be accorded to the terms Father and Mother in relation to biological and social identities). To shift attention to the site of enunciation is to insist that it is not simply the formation of the unconscious that must be theorised but the formation of specific unconsciousnesses, a formation which cannot be divided into social and individual components but which dramatises in each individual case that which is generally unconscious.

If we now return to Pêcheux's division of discursive functions into the pre-constructed and the support-effect, we can indicate how this division, rectified in the light of our criticisms of the Althusser-Pêcheux conception of the unconscious, may well provide one of the starting-points for an investigation of the articulation of the general and specific in the unconscious. It should be noted that Pêcheux's division, as he himself formulates it, resurrects a logic/rhetoric distinction with the support effect understood as the simple substitution of grammatical equivalents (the logical) opposed to the preconstructed which introduces the interferences of the ideological (rhetoric). Thus even from a purely linguistic view there is every reason to be suspicious of the division as it stands. The problem with Pêcheux's interdiscourse is that, like Althusser's policeman, it re-introduces the philosophical subject, coherent and homo-genous, into a Lacanian schema which has as its explicit aim the subversion of that subject. The cost of the re-introduction is clear: the disappearance of the body and desire from the schema. The failure to grasp the radical heterogeneity of the Lacanian Other means that there is nothing left over in that place to function as the object of desire. A first step in the rectification of Pêcheux's position would necessitate a greater emphasis on the other practices imbricated with the interdiscourse and, in particular, the positioning and representation of the body. It is through an emphasis on the body and the impossibility of its exhaustion in its representations that one can understand the material basis with which the unconscious of a discursive formation disrupts the smooth functioning of the dominant ideologies and that this disruption is not simply the chance movement of the signifier but the specific positioning of the body in the economic, political and ideological practices.[13] The analysis of the operations of the preconstructed will thus involve a far more concrete attention to specific ideological and political struggles in which the discur-sive formations are articulated. If the emphasis in the analysis on the preconstructed is on its particular configuration within the social formation, the concept of the support effect must be reworked to take account of those moments where the unrolling of grammatical equivalences is interrupted by the irruption of a desire which can only be read in the specific form which resists any relation of paraphrase.[14]

Notes

1. The first version of this paper was given in November 1976 at the seminar on Social Relations and Discourse organised by Paul Q. Hirst and Sami Zubaida at Birkbeck College, London. I am grateful to those who participated in the discussion there and to Michel Pêcheux for the conversations we had when I was writing the final draft.

2. The standard English translation of Benveniste's term *histoire* is *narrative*. Such a translation loses the force of the French term which combines the sense of history and story. I have therefore retained the French *histoire* and *discours* in my discussion of Benveniste.

3. Accounts of the relations between compound and simple tenses have run into difficulties because they have failed to analyse the two functions of the compound tenses and the way that these distinct functions intersect with the division between *histoire* and *discours*. On the one hand the compound tenses are all 'perfects', that is to say that they all denote an action as 'accomplished' with regard to the 'actual' situation which results from this

accomplishment. As perfects, the compound tenses can occur outside any relations of subordination. But the compound tenses serve a second function which is to indicate anteriority and this anteriority is posed in relation to the corresponding simple form of the verb. This means that in their anterior function the compound tenses can only occur in a subordinate clause for which the main clause uses the corresponding simple form. But the compound tenses find themselves articulated within a double system of relations. While as the tenses denoting 'accomplishment' they find themselves in opposition to the other compound tenses, in expressing 'anteriority' they are simply defined in relation to their corresponding simple form. With this distinction in mind we can understand how the replacement of the aorist by the perfect in speech created certain strains within the tense system. The point of pressure between the aorist and the perfect occurred in the rival first person forms, e.g. *je fis* and *j'ai fait*.

In so far as the realm of *histoire* excludes person then *je fis* is inadmissible in that realm but in so far as it is the aorist it is excluded from the realm of *discours*. There is a slide from the accomplished of the present – *j'ai fait* – to a simple past. But if *discours* thereby gains a temporal distinction it loses a functional distinction.

> In itself, *j'ai fait* is a perfect that furnishes either the form of the perfective or the form of anteriority to the present *je fais*. But when *j'ai fait*, the compound form, becomes the 'aorist of discourse', it takes on the function of the simple form, with the result that *j'ai fait* is sometimes perfect, a compound tense, and sometimes aorist, a simple tense. The system has remedied this difficulty by recreating the missing form. Alongside the simple tense *je fais* is the compound tense *j'ai fait* for the notion of the perfective. Now, since *j'ai fait* slips into the rank of a simple tense, there is a need for a new compound tense that in its turn will express the perfective, this will be the secondary compound *j'ai eu fait*. Functionally *j'ai eu fait* is the new pefect of a *j'ai fait* which has become the aorist. Such is the point of departure for the secondary compound tenses.
>
> (Benveniste 1971: 214–15)

4. The particular process by which the authority of the written is linked specifically to the aorist is peculiar to France, and would have to find further explanation in terms of the ideological and political investment in language during the seventeenth century. In England there is no such evident index of the written although the contemporary growth of the periphrastic tenses and the rise of the novel suggest more complicated links between the grammar of the language and practices of writing.

5. The writing of history is as much a specific practice as that of the novel. The assumption that the past has its own order independently of its present enunciation finds itself challenged in the famous thesis of Walter Benjamin: 'To articulate the past historically does not mean to recognize it "the way it really was" (Ranke). It means to seize hold of a memory as it flashes up at a moment of danger. Historical materialism wishes to retain that image of the past which unexpectedly appears to man singled out by history at a moment of danger' (1970: 257). Such a conception of history will have an evident effect on the distribution of tenses within a particular text.

6. This freedom will often be theorised in terms of its limitations in a variety of sociological perspectives but it is never radically questioned in the posing of subjectivity as an effect of discursivity. Gadet and Pêcheux (1977) offer a comprehensive over-view of the contemporary situation in linguistics.

7. This political thrust of discourse analysis is even more evident (although still not explicit) in the detailed analysis of an article from *Commentary* that Harris published in the same year (1952 b: 474–94).
8. For the sake of clarity I have not emphasised the changes in Pêcheux's position. In fact there is a considerable difference between the *Analyse automatique du discours* (1969) and the two texts of 1975: *les Vérités de la Palice* and 'Mises au point et perspectives de l'analyse automatique du discours' (a text written with the linguist Catherine Fuchs). In particular this involves a shift from the analysis of discourses defined through a sociology of institutions to the analysis of discursive formations defined through the contemporary political and ideological struggles (cf. Pêcheux 1978).
9. Pêcheux's formal method superposes sub-sequences with similar contexts rather than setting up the chain of equivalences. One has then to consider the relation within those sub-sequences which have been grouped together (Haroche, Henry, Pêcheux 1971: 104–5).
10. These criticisms owe much to Jean-Louis Houdebine's review of Pêcheux in *Tel Quel* (1976) and to Pêcheux's own self-criticism which appears as an appendix to the English version of *Les Vérités de la Palice* (1982).
11. 'It is not contestable that logic as the theory of artificial languages in effect developed by taking "natural" language as its original material but one must immediately add that this work always and exclusively aimed to free *mathematics* from the effects of "natural" language (in they way that logic has progressively come to be a part of the domain of mathematics), and not in any way to free *generally* "natural" language itself from its illusions. If not logic would contain within itself all the sciences to turn a remark of Frege, concerning psychology, against himself,' (Pêcheux 1975: 86–7).
12. What Houdebine does not, however, add is that the policeman who has made the mistake is *all the more likely* to give his interpellation a retrospective justification. But to offer this analysis would risk contradicting the major (and indeed only) political thesis of his article, namely that the only agent of repression in France is the French Communist Party.
13. It is through a greater attention to the positioning and representation of the body that Pêcheux would be able to give more political weight to what is politically the most interesting, if theoretically the weakest, section of the book: the discussion of identification. Pêcheux distinguishes three forms of relation to a discursive formation. First, identification (the 'good subject') who assumes without problem the positions offered; then, in direct opposition, counter-identification (the 'bad subject') who identifies him or herself through the refusal of a certain discourse, a refusal which finds itself marked by a variety of grammatical and discursive functions, notably an increased presence of 'shifters': '*Your* social sciences', 'What *you* call liberty', and the deliberate negation in the main clause of an existence that is asserted in the preconstructed of the subordinate clause: 'He who died on the cross to redeem the world never existed.' This position, which could be politically qualified as that of revolt, is essentially defensive but can open onto a third possibility: *disidentification*. It is this concept which is the most vital and least developed part of Pêcheux's work. In it he attempts to describe those practices which displace the agent from that position of subjective centrality which is the result of both identification and counter-identification. These practices are defined as those of science and proletarian politics. Pêcheux's difficulty is that he, quite rightly, finds it impossible to accept a classic science/ideology or proletarian politics/bourgeois politics distinction in which universal and formal features define the divisions. On the

Theoretical essays

other hand Pêcheux remains committed to a *general* description of ideology and bourgeois politics with the result that ideology and bourgeois politics become the eternal hell to which we are subjected and their alternatives are only momentary displacements into a better world. Ideological subjection thus becomes a feature in language while science and proletarian politics are transformed into ephemeral agents of grace which fleetingly rescue us from the sin of the subject position into which we inevitably relapse. The strengths and weaknesses of Pêcheux's position resemble Althusser's. The weakness is the identification of subject and ego, a formulation of the grounds of political and ideological struggle such that defeat is inevitable, the strength is the posing of the problems of identification as politically and ideologically crucial. To rectify the schema offered by Pêcheux it is necessary to stress the incoherence of the interdiscourse, an incoherence grounded in the contradictory positioning and representations of the body. It is in terms of these contradictions that one can provide a material base for an account of the elaboration of specific sciences (there is no need of a general theory of science, simply the specification of the particular developments, which displace and break with the experiential-perceptual centrality of the body). Politically the effect of the emphasis on the body is to stress the importance of a politics of sexuality as the crucial moments in the subversion of the policeman's demand for identification.

14. What is in question here is perhaps the most important of the disidentificatory practices of language which Pêcheux fails to mention: those practices of writing which are generally named as 'literature'. If much literature is devoted to a re-articulation of crucial social identifications, there are certain practices of writing which break definitively with the very possibility of identification. 'Literature' may be limited to certain elites in our class society but its disidentificatory practices on language find wider social currency in certain forms of jokes.

Language, linguistics and the study of literature

If one believes that genesis determines structure, a proposition which a linguist would be likely to dissent from although it is a common premise of literary criticism, then it should be obvious that the two disciplines cannot be considered separately. For if we look back to the first recognisable beginnings of linguistics, we find that they take place in the context of an attempt to establish and comment on literary texts. The scholars of Alexandria in the second century before Christ were motivated in their linguistic enquiry by the changes in the Greek language that had occurred since the literary masterpieces of fifth century Athens had been written. These changes in the language made it difficult to establish what Aeschylus or Sophocles had originally written and what had been interpolated later as an apparently obvious correction necessitated by linguistic change. It was in the context of this practical difficulty, rendered much more acute by the fact that the possibility of historical change in a language was not recognised, and within the theoretical framework provided by the controversy as to whether the basic principle of language was analogy or anomaly, that Dionysos Thrax produced his grammar of Greek. This grammar was predominantly a morphology that set up word-classes. Given that his work was intended as the basis for the establishment of uncorrupted texts, it is unsurprising that its concerns were heavily normative.

If Thrax's efforts were preceded by the linguistic enquiries of Plato, Aristotle and, more valuably, of the Stoics, it is, nevertheless, the case that the vocabulary of cases, tenses and word-classes[1] with which we are familiar is inherited from the Alexandrian scholars of the second century before Christ. Of course,

113

linguistics is not simply grammar. Questions of etymology and phonetics are contemporaneous with the research into grammatical organisation. But it was not until the eighteenth century that etymology was to escape from its determination by concerns extraneous to the systematic organisation of language, an escape that phonetics had made a century earlier.[2]

It is Thrax's grammar which institutes the study of systematic differences in language which is the hallmark of linguistics, even if these systematic differences were given a justification in terms of meaning which weighed heavy on the investigation of the vernacular languages of Europe up until this century and, arguably, weigh heavy still. For example, the distinct inflections of the Latin and Greek verb enable one to refer to distinct tenses. However, these formal differences are interpreted in terms of a particular temporal order and it is this order which is then used to classify other languages even where there is no morphological basis for such an order. The most evident example of this is the classification of a future tense in English. There is no distinct inflection of the verb which expresses actions as taking place in the future and although it is evident that English offers a variety of ways to relate actions to the future, it is arguably preferable to class *will* and *shall* with other modal auxiliaries rather than understanding them in terms of the expression of a pure future.[3]

Indeed if one is impressed by arguments from origin, then it may be worth recalling the similar etymology of *literature* and *grammar* – one of which derives from the Roman word for letter (*littera*) and one from the Greek (*gramme*). But such arguments prove nothing – other than reminding us that our every activity has a history and a name. But it was to more substantial arguments that Roman Jakobson, the legendary Russian linguist, whose work has traversed nearly every important movement in twentieth-century linguistics and whose writing traverses five or six languages, made appeal when, some twenty years ago, he contributed a closing statement to a conference on the relations between literature and language. Jakobson ended his paper with the following remarks: 'All of us here, however, definitely realise that a linguist deaf to the poetic function of language and a literary scholar indifferent to linguistic problems and unconversant with linguistic method are equally flagrant anachronisms' (Jakobson 1960: 377). Jakobson's optimism may seem historically misplaced when the majority of linguists persist in treating literature as a 'deviant' use of language and the majority of literary critics remain blissfully ignorant of current debates around the Extended Standard Theory and its revisions, or of the kinds of considerations of language produced in discussions between those who favour a truth-conditional analysis of meaning and those who would prefer an analysis in terms of speech acts. For twenty years literary critics have been urged to acquaint themselves with linguistic theory and, with rather more shrillness, literary critics have replied that linguists should first learn about language. This particular debate cuts across and confuses that even older debate which determined the institutional structure of literary criticism in the universities – that between the philologists and those who wished to make the study of literature more than a glossary of changes in the language.

What I wish to argue in the later part of this paper is that in so far as Jakobson postulates the two disciplines as distinct, and in so far as co-operation between the two is understood as co-operation between two definite bodies of knowledge, then this is mistaken. That linguistics ignores literature at its peril and that the study and practice of literature is deeply implicated in theories of language will be the argument of this paper. Such a statement does not, however, entail any belief that somehow linguistics and literary criticism should be united, although it may suggest that they should be jointly transformed.

Before, however, turning to the difficult problem of the linguist's theorisation of language and the relation of this to literature, it is necessary to emphasise at some length, and through a series of examples, the centrality of the results produced by linguistic study for any consideration of literature which is to be more than a vapid voluntarism. There is little doubt that our ability to read is dependent on a knowledge of changes in meaning, syntax and phonology and that our ability to analyse is dependent on the possibility of using grammatical and prosodic categories to articulate the literary effects that turn on them.[4] It is perhaps an indication of the parlous state of English as a university course that there are few students or teachers who would quarrel with this statement but there are fewer still who make any effort to understand the basic elements of the synchronic organisation or historical development of English.

Theoretical essays

Of the various fields of language study, it is undoubtedly the historical study of meaning change which is the most relevant to the student of literature and it is an index of the difficulty that meaning poses for contemporary linguistic theory that such a study is no longer an active part of linguistics. Throughout the nineteenth century such study was a fundamental byproduct of the ever increasing sophistication of philological techniques but in this century it has become a neglected, indeed for many linguists a non-existent, area. A recent survey of historical linguistics devoted only two pages to a consideration of meaning change (Bynon 1977) and, at least in England, it is literary critics like William Empson in *The Structure of Complex Words* or Raymond Williams in *Keywords* who have made recent contributions to accounts of historical change.

It is important, however, to recognise that the crucial importance of such studies is not in the restitution of meaning to words that have since fallen out of use but in the reconstitution of the play of possibilities articulated in one word.[5] When Hamlet complains that 'the toe of the peasant comes so near the heel of the courtier he galls his kibe', we are not likely to misread the final phrase even if we have to use a glossary to discover that *kibe* means *chilblains*. If, however, we consider the following speech of Falstaff's from *Henry IV Part 2* we find a more difficult set of problems:

> I have a whole school of tongues in this belly of mine, and not a tongue of them all speaks any other word but my name. And I had but a belly of any indifferency, I were simply the most active fellow in Europe: my womb, my womb, my womb undoes me. Here comes our general.
> (Act IV Scene 3: 18–23.)

If we are surprised by the masculine Falstaff claiming a womb, we may be unsurprised to find a gloss that informs us that *womb*, in this context, means *stomach*. The verb *to womb*, meaning *to enclose an empty space*, gave rise to a series of nominal derivations which included both the sexually unspecific *stomach* as well as the meaning of *uterus* that is current today. It is crucial to a reading of the role of Falstaff to recognise that both meanings were available at the end of the sixteenth century and we should not be surprised at Falstaff's consequent sexual ambiguity, particularly in the context of a claim about the disruption of the

116

normal order of language, 'and not a tongue of them all speaks any other word but my name'.

It is usual to concentrate on the threat to political representation posed by Falstaff but it must be recognised that this threat is more fundamental than any contemporary definitions of the political would suggest. It is not just political representation that Falstaff threatens but representation itself. He subverts linguistic representation by his refusal to treat language in terms of meanings but rather in terms of a constant battle for power between the speakers. Falstaff's rejection of the authority of language threatens the law far more fundamentally than do his express desires. And this threat to the level of representation is embodied in Falstaff's very theatrical presence, marked as he is not in terms of the chronicles that Shakespeare uses to authorise his other characters but as the visible successor to the figure of Vice in the Morality plays. He thus stands for an anachronistic theatrical order which threatens to undermine the more contemporary order that surrounds him. It is not surprising that such a figure should undermine even the possibility of representing sexual difference. Falstaff's body constitutes a polymorphously perverse threat to the possibility of representation. It even claims to undo the arbitrary and social nature of the sign and to speak its own name independently of any social order of language. It is this dislocation of language and the body, occasioned by the deposition of Richard II and the symbolic upheaval which that entails, to which Henry V is addressed as answer across the two parts of *Henry IV*. An essential part of the new order that Henry inaugurates is a re-integration of language and the body. The French princess whom Henry woos at the end of the play is not simply an index of a political union; she bears visible witness to the possibility of re-ordering the body in language, an ordering that is most evident in Act III Scene 4 as her maid Alice names the parts of the body in English and an arbitrary system of signs speak the body rather than the other way round. I am not suggesting that all this can be read out of one quotation but I am suggesting an importance for Falstaff's speech that we would be likely to miss without knowledge of the contemporary meanings of womb.

A knowledge of syntax is as necessary to an ability to grasp the processes of a text as, for example, in the following passage from the Aeolus section of *Ulysses*.

- He spoke on the law of evidence, J.J. O'Molloy said, of Roman justice as contrasted with the earlier Mosaic code, the *lex talionis*. And he cited the Moses of Michelangelo in the Vatican.
- Ha.
- A few wellchosen words, Lenehan prefaced. Silence!
Pause. J.J. O'Molloy took out his cigarette case.
False lull. Something quite ordinary.
Messenger took out his matchbox suddenly and lit his cigar.

I have often thought since on looking back over that strange time that it was that small act, trivial in itself, that striking of that match, that determined the whole aftercourse of both our lives.

(*Ulysses*, Penguin edition, pp. 140–1)

It is in the newspaper headlines and the variety of rhetorics that compose the Aeolus section that the text of *Ulysses* loses any notion of a central meaning. The opening chapters of the book present Stephen or Bloom's thoughts as central but this is no longer the case in the newspaper office. A good example of this displacement can be read in those pages when J.J. O'Molloy is relating the speech made by Seymour Bushe in the Childs murder case. O'Molloy's repetition is punctuated by Stephen's thoughts and descriptions of other events taking place in the office. Many of these events are not linked to Stephen's consciousness and might seem to be recorded by an impersonal narrator, although such a description, which implies a centre for the text which can be located outside the text, is misleading. The lack of a centre becomes the explicit focus of the text as a messenger boy in the office takes out his matchbox and thoughtfully lights his cigar and it is the reflection that follows this action which plays on the syntax of the language to produce its effects. The monotonous repetition of 'that' confronts us with the impossibility of fixing a moment of presence outside language which would ground the text. This impossibility entails not only that the premises of naturalism and realism are incoherent but also that the division between author and text cannot be sustained. The sentence which comments on the striking of the match contains the word 'that' in three distinct grammatical guises. Four of its occurrences are as a demonstrative, but what they demonstrate, in their repetition, is that it is hopeless to link sign and referent outside a system of difference. Each 'that' invites a further 'that' as the world endlessly subdivides into a meaningless catalogue of

118

demonstratives. This ruination of the referential powers of language, similar to processes at work in much modernist writing is emphasised in the occurrence of 'that' as the restrictive relative specifying 'that striking of that match' as 'what determined the whole aftercourse of both our lives'. The function of a restrictive relative clause is to denote a limitation on the reference of the antecedent noun. But in this case the limitation, in its all-embracing nature, is no limitation at all. As the demonstrative increases the power of the microscope of language and the relative produces a telescopic view, the event escapes our control. The sentence provides a perfect example of a controlling metalanguage which promises a position of knowledge to the reader. However, its exaggerated form and its place in the text subvert this promise and delineate the sentence's own structure, the structure of a control that the text is in the process of dissolving. If naturalism assumed the ability to record events without any selection, this sentence demonstrates that events take their place within a selection already operated by language.

The other occurrence of 'that' is to subordinate the indirect statement to 'I have often thought'. The difficulty, however, is to locate the referent of the 'I'. Is this Stephen Dedalus as the future author he is to become looking back on the significance of a particular event? Such a belief would have to rest on the realist assumption that there are significant moments in a life. This position, unfortunately, is undermined by the facts of language that the text is forcing on our attention. If the description of an event can always by further differentiated then it becomes impossible to isolate a moment in the past to which significance can be attributed. To describe the past is not to map language against reality but to seek reality in the significant repetitions that bear witness to our constitution. Stephen Dedalus and James Joyce cannot be held apart: neither one is the cause of the other. As we read through *Ulysses* it becomes impossible to separate character and author.

As a final example of how both syntactic analysis and lexical knowledge are essential to even the most basic notions of reading a text, we can consider the famous passage in Book 1 of *Paradise Lost* which describes Satan moving towards the shore and then looking over his defeated army:

He scarce had ceas't when the superior Fiend
Was moving toward the shore; his ponderous shield
Ethereal temper, massy, large and round,
Behind him cast; the broad circumference
Hung on his shoulders like the Moon, whose Orb
Through Optic glass the *Tuscan* Artist views
At Ev'ning from the top of *Fesole*,
Or in *Valdarno*, to descry new Lands,
Rivers, or Mountains in her spotty Globe.
His Spear, to equal which the tallest Pine
Hewn on *Norwegian* hills, to be the Mast
Of some great Ammiral, were but a wand,
He walk't with to support uneasy steps
Over the burning Marl, not like those steps
On Heaven's Azure, and the torrid Clime
Smote on him sore besides, vaulted with Fire;
Nathless he so endur'd, till on the Beach
Of that inflamed Sea, he stood and call'd
His Legions, Angel Forms, who lay intrans't
Thick as Autumnal Leaves that strow the Brooks
In *Vallombrosa*, where th'*Etrurian* shades
High overarch't imbow'r; or scatter'd sedge
Afloat, when with fierce Winds *Orion* arm'd
Hath vext the Red-Sea Coast, whose waves o'erthrew
Busiris and his *Memphian* Chivalry,
While with perfidious hatred they persu'd
The Sojourners of *Goshen*, who beheld
From the safe shore thir floating Carcasses
And broken Chariot Wheels; so thick bestrown
Abject and lost lay these ...

Paradise Lost, 1: 283–312

The entire sequence produces a continual changing of perspective, common to Milton's description of Hell in which metaphor and simile follow one another so quickly that there is no question of a basic description which the equivalences or comparisons elaborate. Instead the description simply becomes the passage through these comparisons and equivalences, a *transport*, to give metaphor its original force, of language. The comparisons that elaborate 'his Legions, Angel Forms' engage a constant change of perspective which turns on the seemingly infinite number of subordinate clauses and the heterogeneity of the literary references that Milton employs. The opening disjunction opposes the leaves that strew the brooks at Vallombrosa to the sedge which is scattered on the Red Sea. The interest of the disjunction is not simply one of scale, from a brook to a sea, but also of literary genre: the relative 'where th'Etrurian shades/High overarcht imbowr' and the adverbial 'when with fierce winds Orion armd/ Hath vext the Red-Sea Coast' juxtapose the world of pastoral with that of classical epic while the relative which qualifies Red-Sea Coast introduces an Old Testament reference.[6] The complex pattern of subordination refuses any possibility of ordering the variety of references and it is not until after a further adverbial clause of time that a relative clause 'who beheld from the safe shore' provides the reader with a point of rest and vision. In this delay of a point of identification, in this rejection of a standard world of literary reference, Milton forces the reader to refuse any of the particular representations of the fallen angels in order that he may construct the truth of their situation. The necessary presupposition of Milton's poetic practice is an epistemology in which truth can actually reside in the processes of language and not simply in an external world which language is called to represent. Two such epistemologies were available in the Renaissance and although theoretically separate they were often combined.[7] The hermetic philosophers of the Renaissance evolved a theory in which language and the world were articulated together in a system of correspondences which allowed the possibility of finding relations between things inscribed in the language. Such theories often found their ultimate support in a conception of both the world and language as the product of God's wit. A more specifically religious theory of the truth to be found in language was provided by St Augustine. For Augustine, the redemption was also a redemption of language and if normal uses of language were arbitrary and excluded from any direct contact with truth, certain figurative uses of language did allow access to the realm of divine truth. Both theories were under political, ideological and religious attack at the time *Paradise Lost* was written; this attack finding institutional form in the Royal Society. One of the Society's most important functions was to promulgate a theory of language which destroyed the possibility of truth residing in language except in so far as language functioned as representation.

It is in the light of that contemporary ideological debate that one can consider the reference at the opening of the passage to Galileo, the 'Tuscan Artist'. If one looks at a standard gloss, it will simply carry the information that *artist* means *scientist*. While it is true that art and its derivatives still have that Renaissance meaning which covers every intellectual activity (and would, therefore, include what we now call science), it is important to recognise that elements of our current meaning which opposes art to science were developing at this time. Thus the first mention of such a meaning in the OED comes in 1678 – just a decade after the first publication of *Paradise Lost* – when a manual on making sun dials records, 'Though we may justly account Dyalling originally a Science yet ... it is now become to many of the ingenious no more difficult than an Art'. It would be dangerous to read this entry as using our current meaning of science, a development of the early nineteenth century, but it is significant that it opposes a realm of inquiry that can produce truth (science) to a mere practice which has no epistemological status (art).

At this point a linguist might quite reasonably interject that this is all very interesting and demonstrates how analyses of literature draw on studies in lexis and grammar but it has nothing to say to linguistics itself. For what is crucial to the establishment of linguistics is the specification within the heterogeneous material of language of a definite object which linguistics studies. Famously it was de Saussure who accomplished such a specification and, at the risk of pedantry, it is worth reviewing Saussure's argument both to understand the linguist's objection but also to indicate how the objection only has force within the realm of syntax and that the object which he considers his own dissolves once one considers problems of meaning.

The major concept which Saussure develops is that of linguistic value. It is from this concept of value that all the other major Saussurean concepts (*langue/parole*, signifier/signified, diachrony/synchrony, syntagm/paradigm) follow one after another.[8] The problem that obsessed Saussure was simple; how could one say that two occurences of the same word were the same word? And if one could not, how could linguistics claim to be a science when it could not identify its most basic objects? If I call a meeting to order by saying 'Gentlemen, Gentlemen', how can I claim that both words are the same when the pronunciation or intonation may be different? The problem can be dissolved once one recognises that what is at stake is a relational and not a material identity. This opposition can be grasped through Saussure's famous example of the 8.45 express from Geneva to Paris. What enables us to refer to this train is not a set of material identities – each day the train is made up of engines and coaches which are different – but the relational identity that it is given in the timetable – it is not the 8.30 for Lausanne or the 9.00 for Geneva. (Saussure 1974: 108–9)

Certain consequences follow immediately from this notion of relational identity. Linguistics is not concerned with the positive characteristics of particular realisations of language but with the differential structure which allows those particular productions. It is this distinction that Saussure captures in his terms *langue* and *parole*. *Langue* refers to the specific set of systematic differences which allows the production of particular utterances of *parole*.

A linguist's reasons for professing lack of interest in the readings of Shakespeare, Milton and Joyce would turn on conceptions of *langue* – it might be argued that, whatever their incidental interest, they had nothing to say about linguistics' object of study. But whereas this is true in the case of syntax – the analyses do not reflect back on the syntactic distinctions they use – it is emphatically not the case at the level of meaning – where the examples produced do not just analyse specific uses of particular meanings but constitute those meanings in the analysis. Thus in Milton's use of the word *Artist*, it is not a question of specifying a meaning and then a use but rather of an account in which that meaning is in the process of changing as a word gets articulated in new, or in opposition to new, discourses. And the description and specification of these discourses will never be purely linguistic but will necessitate an account of the institutional sites of language use, an account which will draw on a wide variety of facts and interpretations. The idea that there is an organisation of meaning which belongs to *langue*, and the analysis of which might be termed semantics, and separable uses of that organisation, which might be analysed under the various rubrics of pragmatics, socio-linguistics or stylistics, merely reproduces a distinction between logic and rhetoric, endemic to our thinking about language since the seventeenth century, which opposes an order of language determined by its relation to

123

the order of things and another order, deemed inferior on this account, determined by its relation to the speaker. Such a distinction inevitably forces linguistics away from the study of language in its specificity and towards a mythical logic or psychology which will provide this universal ordering of meaning independently of specific uses of language.

It is at this point that the difficulty of simply proposing some institutional union of the disciplines of linguistics and literary criticism becomes apparent, for the difficulties of analysing meaning necessitate a recasting of both disciplines. Saussure's concept of value signalled, above all, a break with the primacy of meaning in specifying the object of linguistics. But Saussure himself allowed for the possibility of using the concept of linguistic value to analyse meaning. This decision indicates the extent to which Saussure himself underestimated his own theoretical achievement.[9] His belief in the possibility of analysing meaning linguistically is in contradiction with that impulse which led him to formulate the concept of linguistic value as a strategy for dislocating meaning from the field of linguistics. If it is perfectly legitimate to divorce the language from its situation in order to study phonology, morphology and syntax where differences of situation contribute only secondary characteristics – it is impossible to perform the same operation at the level of meaning where the relations of the meanings of a text to its socio-historical conditions (of both production and reception) are not secondary but constitutive. In short there is no such entity as *langue* at the level of meaning. And indeed, strictly speaking, there is no such thing as meaning in so far as the term assumes an entity independent of the different ideological, political or theoretical positions which inform language and the different institutional conditions of utterance. It is not that a word has different meanings for different speakers but that the same lexical item appears in different discourses.

If Saussure refused to allow meaning a position of centrality within linguistics, he retained a belief in its existence. That he failed to see the way in which at the level of meaning language is always discourse can be explained in terms of the two great lacunae of Saussure's theory: subjectivity and institutions. For Saussure there was no question but that the speaker's relation to his utterances was one of transparency. If the functioning of *langue* was unconscious and to be located in some notion of community, this functioning was simply at the service of the conscious intentions of the speaker. It was to this area of conscious intentionality that *parole* referred. The idea that we might produce meanings of which we were not conscious, that the workings of discourse and desire made our own speech as much material for interpretation as a foreign language is alien to the *Course in General Linguistics*. This belief in the transparency of the speaking subject is complemented by an inability to conceive of institutions as other than straightforward means for achieving ends that could be separately and naturally defined. This is made clear in another famous passage where he distinguishes *langue* from any other social institutions in the following terms:

> Other human institutions – customs, laws, etc. – are all based in varying degrees on the natural relations of things; all have of necessity adapted the means employed to the ends pursued. Even dress in fashion is not entirely arbitrary; we can deviate only slightly from the conditions dictated by the human body. Language is limited by nothing in the choice of means, for apparently nothing would prevent the association of any idea whatsoever with just any sequence of sounds. (Saussure 1974: 75–6)

This rather naive view – that there is a determinate, evident and natural relationship between means and ends in institutions – complements the belief in a full subjectivity which simply uses the resources of *langue* in *parole*. Sixty years after Saussure's death, with both the variety of Marxist or sociological analyses which refuse such transparency to institutions and the discoveries of psychoanalysis which make clear the complexity of the subject's relation to language, it is impossible to understand language either as a transparent medium for individual expression or as a simple medium for communication within an institution whose functioning can be exhaustively described in the natural relationship of things.

In order to deal with the effects of meaning we must combine an analysis of the institutional sites of language together with an analysis of subjectivity in language to enable us to understand how specific practices of language both produce subject positions for individuals and articulate various practices within institutions. This statement may seem both blunt and unspecific but it is

125

possible to give it some gloss (and one that will indicate the consequent transformation of linguistics and literary criticism) by considering and recasting one of the most influential characterisations of language in relation to literature – that provided by Jakobson in the paper already quoted from at the beginning of this article. Jakobson argued that any speech event could be analysed in terms of six linguistic functions:

> An outline of these functions demands a concise survey of the constitutive factors in any speech event, in any act of verbal communication, the ADDRESSER sends a MESSAGE to the ADDRESSEE. To be operative the message requires a CONTEXT referred to ('referent' in another, somewhat ambiguous, nomenclature), seizable by the addressee, and either verbal or capable of being verbalised; a CODE fully, or at least partially, common to the addresser and addressee (or in other words, to the encoder and decoder of the message); and, finally, a CONTACT, a physical and psychological connection between the addresser and the addressee, enabling both of them to enter and stay in communication. (Jakobson 1960: 358)

Each of these factors relates to a particular function of language: Addresser (*Emotive*), Addressee (*Conative*), Context (*Referential*), Code (*Metalingual*), Contact (*Phatic*) and, finally, Message (*Poetic*). The first five functions are perhaps evidently related to the relevant factors. They distinguish between the message's primary aims: to express the speaker's state of mind, to influence the addressee(s), to refer to some third element, to comment on the meaning of what is being said, or to establish that the message is being received. The sixth function is defined by Jakobson as a message which reflects on its own structure, the moment at which paradigmatic choices influence syntagmatic ones, or, to use his own words: 'The poetic function projects the principle of equivalence from the axis of selection into the axis of combination'.

Jakobson's whole analysis into factors and functions rests on an implicit appeal to a notion of *langue* functioning at the level of meaning as well as that of syntax and phonology (although it might be said that almost all the specific analyses in the paper concentrate on the phonological and the syntactic). If we refuse this assumption, which posits individual speakers in a common relation to a totality, then much of the analysis dissolves.

If we select the institutional sites of language as the starting point of our analysis rather than some notion of *langue* as a totality then, for example, addresser and addressee become functions of the variety of places allocated to the speaker in a discourse rather than basic elements given by syntax or pragmatics. Such a focus will also emphasise how it is impossible to split off some general referential function of language. Every particular discursive formation has its own methods of specifying and referring to the extra-discursive. It may be one of the continuing weaknesses of contemporary philosophies of language to imagine that these methods can be unified under some general principle. In each case there will be a complex of practices and discourses within which reference will take place and it is not possible to talk of some general relation between language and context while ignoring the specific practices with which the language is imbricated. The history of sciences is particularly rich in such examples: when Galileo referred to the evidence for his theory of the solar system, the reference was dependent, amongst other things, on the acceptance of the operations of the telescope. It is impossible to abstract language from conditions of verification in order to pose some general theory of reference.

It is only if we understand the complexity of the varieties of methods of referring (and one might hesitate to gather them under the general term of reference) that we can theorise the way in which the very positions of addresser and addressee may be transformed by a system of reference. Jakobson's model presupposes a simple and uncomplicated three person model of language in which syntactic and discursive distinctions coincide. The references that I make to a third person are theorised in such a way that they could have no effectivity on the fundamental and given positions of addresser and addressee. Much of the functioning of fictional forms, particularly the novel, can, however only be understood as the reworking of the positions of addresser and addressee across a series of third person statements.

The point of these considerations is to suggest that there is no universal ordering of factors and functions of language that we can specify in advance. If there are certain general concerns which have been useful to date in analysing discourse, this does not mean that it is possible to exhaustively enumerate features of language in advance of particular investigations. As has been argued, it is not clear that the particular methods by which a variety of discursive formations produce and allow evidence can be brought together under the head of reference. And these considerations also affect the consideration of the notion of a metalingual function. If, at the level of meaning, there is no unified structure of language then there is even less a metalanguage which can specify those meanings. Once again, as in the case of reference, each discursive formation is very likely to have a specific set of rules for producing paraphrases and equivalences but it is precluding the investigation to decree in advance that these will provide an identical function. Even the phatic function cannot be simply universalised depending as it does on a complex series of institutional practices in, for example, law or science. One of the conclusions of these arguments is that there is no reason why every utterance or even the idealisation of certain forms of utterance will be investigable at this level. If we refuse to allow the existence of *langue* at the level of meaning then we must not shirk the consequences that only certain utterances will be amenable to analysis. Once again we will be faced with Saussure's problem of identifying the units for analysis and this will be a task which cannot be universalised across the whole language.

If we now finally turn to the poetic function it is clear that we must consider it not as a universal feature of language but rather in terms of the rules within and across certain discourses which allow paradigmatic choices to interrupt and reflect on syntagmatic organisation. It is possible to consider discourses that have very rigorous operations to prevent such operations and others which don't (not to forget that third possibility: discourses to which such a characterisation is simply not pertinent). Such a position might allow us to isolate literature as an institution whose changing material determinates do not affect a unity to be discerned in a peculiar privilege given to that aspect of language which Jakobson names the poetic.

So far it has been an implicit assumption that institutions and discourses have total autonomy and that one can postulate some homologous relation between them. This is, of course, not the case. Institutions overlap and conflict, discourses are not tied in some obviously physical way to their institutional sites. Indeed the very possibility of discursive transformation rests on these contradictory relations. It is here that there is another crucial change of emphasis from the beautiful listing of institutions and discourses and then their correlation, rather they will find their origin in some contemporary area of institutional and discursive change and contradiction and it is here that the determination of regularities in the corpus will be grounded. The argument that it is the situation of the investigator which is the final determinant of the forms and grounds of argument may sound alarmingly unscientific. Whatever its epistemological status, and this could be argued for, it should not alarm any analyst of literature because it has consistently been claimed that it is such forms of argument that distinguish English as a discipline. And it has been within the discipline of English that many of the most penetrating studies of language, in the form that I describe it, have taken place. Richards, Empson and, more recently, Raymond Williams have contributed a great deal to the study of language in this century. But it is a contribution that has often been ignored by linguistics. One of the major reasons for this has been a certain failure by this tradition, which could ironically be termed a Cambridge one, to consider rigorously the relation between their own work and the dominant schools of linguistics. It should now be clear that such a consideration would not be a prologomenon to some pious institutional union between linguistics and literary criticism but to an analysis of language which would recast the assumptions and disciplines of linguistics and literary criticism.

Notes

1. The adjective is the only important word-class not identified by the Greeks. Its different status from the noun was only properly recognised with the detailed study of Romance languages.
2. Before these dates phonetics had been dogged by the belief that a straightforward correspondence between letters and sounds could be realised and etymology by the failure to understand the principles of historical change in language.
3. For the details of this argument see Barbara Strang (1968: 162–170). For a statement of the more classical analysis of 'will' and 'shall' see Otto Jespersen. It should be noted that even in English it is not simply the future tense which is organised differently from the Latin. Sentences such as 'If I loved her, I'd send her flowers' suggest that what we traditionally call the past tense of the verb is an inflection which cannot be fully semantically analysed in terms of tense.
4. Phonetics and phonology present so many special problems that I am not going to consider them in this paper. My personal view, however, is that there are fundamental universal questions about sound in language. Any work in this area would have to take as its starting point the work of I. Fónagy,

Theoretical essays

Die Metaphern in der Phonetik (1963) and the second section of Julia Kristeva's *La Révolution du langage poétique* (1974), particularly the chapter entitled 'Rythmes phoniques et sémantiques' pp. 209–64. Independently of any theoretical questions, the fact that many students and teachers of literature have not the faintest idea how the poetry or prose they study would have sounded if read aloud at the time of its composition is a practically unparalleled example of scholastic blindness.

5. Perhaps the best analysis of the play of possibilities available within a single word is Empson's analysis of Pope's use of 'wit' in the *Essay on Criticism* in *The Structure of Complex Words* (1977: 84–100).

6. If one considers the literary history of this simile, then Milton's use of it to heterogenise the range of literary references beyond the epic becomes even more evident. There is a useful account of its history in epic in C. M. Bowra *From Virgil to Milton* (1945: 240–1).

7. For a short summary of these two positions see Geoffrey Shepherd's introduction to his edition of Sidney's *An Apology for Poetry* (1973: 56–7).

8. For a brilliant account of the centrality of Saussure's concept of value see Oswald Ducrot (1968: 44–9).

9. For a more detailed statement of this argument see Cl. Haroche, P. Henry, M. Pêcheux (1971).

Realism: Balzac and Barthes

In memoriam Michel Pêcheux

> They told me, Heraclitus, they told me you were dead,
> They brought me bitter news to hear and bitter tears to shed.
> I wept, as I remembered, how often you and I
> Had tired the sun with talking and sent him down the sky.

My topic today is realism because realism focuses a fundamental relation between language and literature, and, in so doing, engages with a problem to which this conference finds itself returning again and again. In brief the problem runs as follows: how can we give an account of the reality of our signifying practices (from science to small talk) which does not reduce them to the reflection of an anterior real but which, at the same time, when it analyses the changes and transformations of those signifying practices, gives sufficient weight to a reality never exhausted by signification.

In posing this problem one is also addressing this conference under its two contradictory aspects. Of course, there is always more than one contradiction running through any institutional and discursive event as massive as this one, but it seems obvious to me that the primary contradiction is that we are all gathered here because of certain political commitments, particularly commitments to cultural politics, and yet, at the same time, we are almost all dependent for our presence here on the positions we occupy within our different national educational institutions.

It is too easy, however, to attempt to elide this contradiction by stressing one side or the other − 'What this should really be is a political conference', the dream of some purely political project which would bring us together, or 'This is just academic' as though one could possibly accept the self-definitions of the academy. What brings us together from our varied national positions is, above all, the shared reading of a series of texts and the contradictory insertion/intervention of that reading in various different national cultures and politics. The texts in question, the canon, is familiar to us all. But it is itself marked by this familiar contradiction. If a series of books produced in Paris in the sixties continue to reverberate around the universities of the western world and to play a determining part in many of the debates within the humanities and the human sciences, such reverberations are political as well as academic. There is, of course, the obvious political effect of these texts within academic institutions ; institutions which contribute to the reproduction and transformation of social relations by producing a wide variety of discourses and by a series of trainings so crucial to the differentiation of society. But the texts are not simply political in the moment of their reception, they are, as importantly and probably more importantly, political as well as academic in the moment of their production. For they take part in that movement for which May '68 is an extremely misleading shorthand, and which still has to be understood in all its continental and intercontinental complexity. Such an evaluation is not merely a matter of theoretical work, it is something which engages us in the most hidden as well as the most public of our acts. It is my own profound conviction that such an evaluation is the only possible basis from which to oppose the current ideological dominance of the right. I stress the word 'possible' for when the evaluation is completed (and *when* rather than *if* is already optimistic), there is no guarantee that it will aid us in the struggles to which our unnatural flesh is heir.

At the intellectual level, whether Althusser, Lacan and Derrida will come to seem merely historical curiosities – scholarly footnotes in studies on the influence of Marx, Freud and Heidegger – or whether their thought will prove genuinely fruitful, is still difficult to determine, caught as one still is between the excitement of a moment when the categories of meaning and being seemed in fundamental re-alignment and a rather longer term period in which the efforts to understand the relations between subjectivity, sexuality and sociality appear to be paralysed in formalist repetitions. It is this formalism which very largely now seems, particularly in an Anglo-American context, to occupy the space

132

of *Theory*, a word which I must personally confess jars more every time I hear it and jars all the more because it is pronounced in a tone of political piety which seems inappropriate in every way. Theory is important in so far as it can help us to answer certain pressing problems, problems which erupt in our lives whether we like it or not, problems of politics, sexuality and race, and which we attempt to theorise through concepts of class, gender and culture. It is here that theory and its inevitable concern with representation, with the relation between fact and concept, has its part to play. Theory cannot, however, be an end in itself outside some modern self-deluding version of aestheticism or some traditional self-serving version of careerism.

In an effort to contribute to that general evaluation of the late sixties I have chosen as a text Roland Barthes's *S/Z*. The written trace of a seminar held in the years 1968 and 1969, *S/Z* is the text which focuses, for me, the strengths and weaknesses of that period in an intellectual form.

It is Barthes's choice of a story to analyse which determines Balzac's place in the title of this paper but it would be a mistake to think that Barthes's choice was aleatory. If the immediate occasion for the selection of Balzac's story *Sarrasine* was an article by Jean Reboul in *Cahiers pour l'analyse* and some fleeting comments of Bataille's, it is also the case that to analyse a story by Balzac is to engage with traditional Marxist definitions of the novel. Is it not Balzac that Engels praises as the most complete guide to the reality of France in the post-Napoleonic era (Marx and Engels 1976: 91–2)? Is it not Balzac who functions for Lukács as one of the key figures in the elaboration of the crucial terms for the debate about realism?

> The question arises whether it is the unity of the external and internal worlds or the separation between them which is the social basis of the greatness of a novel; whether the modern novel reached its culminating point in Gide, Proust and Joyce or had already reached its peak much earlier, in the works of Balzac and Tolstoy; so that today only individual great artists struggling against the current — as for instance Thomas Mann — can reach the heights already long attained. (Lukács 1950: 2)

In this Marxist debate between ancient and modern, Barthes with his championing of *le nouveau roman* had already placed himself on the side of the modern. His earlier work, *Le Degré zéro de l'écriture* and *Mythologies* had, however, continued to accept the Marxist definition of 1848 as the watershed before which the bourgeoisie were able to express their universal aspirations with good conscience but, after which, the European-wide revolutions had made clear the class limitations of those universal ideals. Indeed, in many ways, *Mythologies* sought to explain the signifying mechanisms which enabled the bourgeoisie to transform the limiting features of their culture into irreducible facts of nature. These operations which Barthes termed *myth* ensured that the processes of signification were ignored in favour of a reality thereby produced as always already brute and always already given.

By the mid-sixties, however, Barthes oscillated between considering the operations of myth and the consequent denial of the processes of signification as the central feature of bourgeois culture, and a more radical view which analysed this occultation of the sign as fundamental to a western concern with representation which went back to the Greeks and which post-Renaissance Europe had merely accentuated. In challenging the very terms of representation, Barthes was taking issue not simply with Lukács's evaluation of ancient and modern but with his characterisation of the opposition in terms of the relation between internal and external worlds.

These concerns were illuminatingly set out in a short article entitled 'L'effet du réel' which Barthes published in *Communications* in 1968 and the composition of which was presumably contemporary with the beginning of the seminar which was to produce *S/Z*.[1] The majority of the article is taken up with considering part of the description of Madame Aubain's room in *Un Coeur simple* when Flaubert writes that 'un vieux piano supportait, sous un baromètre, un tas pyramidal de boîtes et de cartons' (Flaubert 1965: 28) ('Under a barometer stood an old piano loaded with a pyramid of boxes and cartons'). Barthes starts from the puzzle of how we are to account for the information that this description contains? For anyone concerned with the structural analysis of narrative such sentences seem simply redundant. They do not contribute to the narrative development and they cannot be integrated into a wider thematic function. If the piano might conceivably be analysed as an indicator of social function and the boxes and cartons as a sign of disorder within the *maison* Aubain, it is impossible to attach a signification to the barometer which appears like a stain of insignificance in the text. What is the significance, Barthes asks, of this insignificance? And it is to that question that the article addresses itself.

Description has long been a feature of western writing but it has always been governed by certain laws of genre. No such generic conventions govern the descriptions within the nineteenth-century text. Barthes refuses to accept the standard explanation that the laws of genre have been replaced by the features of reality itself. The examination of Flaubert's endless rewriting of the description of the town of Rouen in *Madame Bovary* reveals, for Barthes, that Flaubert has no concern with the reality of Rouen but, rather, with the reality of his own style. For Barthes the descriptions of Rouen are not governed by the narrative of the book but by the general function of representation which works on the basis of a double refusal. On the one hand representation refuses to accept the unlimited nature of the real, a nature which entails that no description can be brought to an end, while, on the other, it refuses to acknowledge the operations of fantasy in the description by supposedly grounding the writing in external conditions. The representation that is left after this double operation seems to resist meaning, to display its own insignificance. But this insignificance merely reduplicates the mythic opposition, which Barthes finds central to bourgeois culture, between the intelligible and the lived. And this brute concrete element of the lived, this barometer, exists within the novel as a guarantee that the intelligibility that the novel articulates is not in fact an articulation, for, like the barometer, it rests exterior to the text. Barthes contrasts this novelistic relation with the relation between the real and the *vraisemblable* in classical culture which defined intelligibility in terms of the *exclusion* of the real. Barthes continues: 'Par là-même, il y a rupture entre le vraisemblable ancien et le réalisme moderne; mais par là-même aussi, un nouveau vraisemblable naît, qui est précisément le réalisme (entendons par là tout discours qui accepte des énonciations créditées par le seul référent)' (Barthes 1968: 88). ('By that very fact there is a break between the old *vraisemblable* and modern realism but by that same fact a new *vraisemblable* is born which is, precisely, realism (let us understand by that term any discourse which accepts enunciations guaranteed by the referent alone.')

At a more technical level Barthes analyses the operation as the abolition of the signified so that the signifier is placed in direct relation to the referent in a movement which seems to escape all questions of meaning. But we should not think thereby that we escape meaning; what is in question in this whole operation is the production of a meaning, the absence of signification signifies direct contact with the real: 'car dans le moment même où ces détails sont réputés dénoter directement le réel, ils ne font rien d'autre, sans le dire, que le signifier' (Barthes 1968: 88). ('Because in the very moment when these details are held to denote the real directly, they do nothing except, without admitting it, to signify it'.)[2] Barthes's task in *S/Z*, which is implicitly set out in the article, is to unmask the operations of the realist text: to rework all questions of the referent in terms of the signified. The weakness of this position, which is not to say that it does not have strengths, can be briefly indicated by arguing that the setting of Rouen is an absolutely central feature of *Madame Bovary* − it is the juxtaposition of an adulterous love affair and a provincial town which made the book so shocking on its appearance. The historical point can be made theoretically by arguing that the passage to the referent always engages the signified and that Barthes's dream of a bracketing out of the referent presupposes a unity of language which does not apply when there is any question of specific practices of writing.

Before turning in detail to these questions, however, I would like to summarise briefly the procedures of *S/Z*. Barthes analyses Balzac's story line by line fracturing the text into five codes in which each fragment participates and whose interweaving composes the text. The codes are not strict rules of paradigmatic and syntagmatic substitution and, in that, Barthes distances himself from those in the sixties who wished to produce a universal grammar of narrative. Much structural analysis of narrative before Barthes had attempted to read texts as instantiations of structures which existed independently of their textual realisation. Barthes, conscious of the dialectic between reader and text, refused to locate the codes immanently within the text but in the relation of reading. But if the codes are the result of the interests that the analyst brings to the text, they are not, therefore, to be located in some subjective voluntarism; it is not the analyst's choice any more than the author's consciousness or the text's identity that guarantee the codes, rather it is a particular set of operations: 'Je ne suis pas caché dans le texte, j'y suis seulement irrepérable: ma tâche est de mouvoir, de translater des systèmes dont le prospect ne s'arrête ni au texte ni à 'moi', opératoirement, les sens que je trouve sont avérés, non par 'moi' ou d'autres, mais par leur marque *systématique*: il n'y a pas d'autre *preuve* d'une lecture que la qualité et l'endurance de sa systématique; autrement dit: que son fonctionnement' (Barthes: 1970 a: 17). ('I am not hidden in the text, I am simply irrecoverable from it: my task is to move, to shift systems whose perspective ends neither at the text or with me, the meanings I find are confirmed, not by me or by others but by their systematic mark: there is no other proof of a reading than the quality and endurance of its systematic; in other words: than its functioning.')

Barthes's comments indicate how the repetitions analysed in the text find their validity within a process of interpretation which is social. What is not allowed any determination in that functioning is the social practices which constitute the moment of the text's production.

The story itself starts with a description of a ball in fashionable Paris. The narrator who is describing the scene is drawn into the action when a mysterious aged figure appears in whom the narrator's partner becomes inordinately interested. The narrator wishes to seduce his partner and promises to tell her the story of this figure in exchange for the promise of an affair. It is this story which is the story of Sarrasine, a sculptor who goes to Rome and falls in love with a singer called Zambinella. What Sarrasine does not know is that women's roles in these operas are taken by castrated men. The story of Sarrasine is the story of this discovery and Sarrasine's subsequent death. The figure at the ball is this same Zambinella now very old. The story so horrifies the young woman that she renounces all thoughts of a sexual affair.

Barthes's five codes into which he analyses the text are as follows:

Proairetic code
This code is the code of actions and its name is derived from the term Aristotle uses in his analysis of actions: *proairesis*. It refers

to the logic of actions that make up a text. Thus, in a famous example, when in a Bond novel a phone rings there is an expectation that it will be answered. It is these sequences which can be endlessly expanded – 'The phone rang. He hesitated for a moment and then answered' – which contribute in large part to the 'realism' of the text.

Hermeneutic code
This is the code which refers to the plot or the enigma – to the text's production of a mystery which it then resolves. In *Sarrasine* the fundamental enigma is the identity of the figure who appears at the ball – an identity revealed to us by the gradual unfolding of the text. It is this unfolding, across a series of delays and false expectations, which constantly invites the reader to read further.

Semic code
This is the code which collects together those parts of the text that might appear in a thematic reading. Thus, in *Sarrasine*, for example, the moon recurs in a variety of different contexts. In some ways this code would correspond to certain kinds of impressionistic literary critical readings.

The analysis of these three codes: the code of *actions*, the code of *enigmas* and the code of *themes* contributes much to our understanding of narratives. It serves, in some sense, as a particularly succinct and brilliant summary of the previous decade's work on the structural analysis of narratives. But it is the other two codes which are both original and more problematic because they pose more clearly questions of the text's production and reception – on the one hand the systems of distribution, the standards of literacy, the forms of economic relations in which the text first appeared, and, on the other, those same forms in their contemporary operation with special emphasis on the forms of education and commerce which produce the text in the present in an active relation with its contemporary readers.

Cultural or Referential Code
This is the code which refers to the general area of cultural and historical knowledges; it ransacks a whole series of contemporary sciences and ideologies and weaves them into the text. The

political and economic situation in France, the cultural and political milieu in Rome – the list proliferates endlessly. For Barthes this code can be fully understood in terms of the positioning of the reader in an already ordained position of knowledge. It is this code which, 150 years after the text's production, we often need to relearn but which would have been readily available to Balzac's audience. It must be emphasised that it is not a question of what Balzac's audience knew, but their understanding of the positions from which knowledge was to be produced. What is significant about the references is that they are understood as references to accepted knowledges. They thus figure a position of knowledge which is occupied by both text and reader.

Symbolic code

This is the most important and problematic of the codes not least because, in this case more than any other, code is a misleading word. The symbolic does not refer, as it does in its most common English meaning, to a set of symbols which represent other entities across a grid of interpretation. Instead it is understood (following Lévi-Strauss and Lacan) in terms of the whole field in which symbols are produced – the very possibility of representing one thing by another. The symbolic thus refers to the processes which render representation possible, most importantly and centrally in language. On this reading the symbolic is conceived as the articulation of a series of differences which inaugurate both identity and language. The world is rendered into identities by the very process of representation. The rendering of identities and the signifying practice of language are, on this account, *one and the same process*. The symbolic code is thus the space of the investigation of difference and signification. Centrally in the Balzac text, it is articulated around sexual difference and the problem of sexual difference posed by Zambinella. Both male and female s/he collapses difference and identity on the most crucial of sites: the body. Zambinella's very existence poses a threat to any possibility of representation and this threat runs through every level of the text where all the means of representation seem on the point of a vertiginous collapse: money, language, painting and indeed the text itself become unreliable and arbitrary as world and language, difference and signification are unravelled by a sexuality that cannot be determined in its identity.

Theoretical essays

In his opening remarks Barthes writes: 'il faut, à la fois, dégager le texte de son extérieur et de sa totalité' (Barthes 1970a: 12). ('It is necessary, at one and the same time, to disengage the text from its exterior and its totality'.) This comment refuses any reading in terms of either a sociology or a psychology and thus refuses the very terms of Lukács's definition of realism, which would try to locate texts in either external or internal worlds. For Barthes, the novel is only connotation, denotation is defined away until it is only the final connotation within the realist text, functioning as an alibi for the activities of language. Reality is no longer external or internal, social or psychological but linguistic and textual. In marking this displacement Barthes used a different theoretical vocabulary in the book than that employed in the earlier article. Whereas he had earlier talked of signifier, signified and referent, in *S/Z* denotation and connotation become the major focus of the early theoretical preliminaries. In both cases denotation and the referent have the same function: the illusory guarantor of the innocence of language; the disavowal of both the multiplicity of the real and the insistence of fantasy.

Many of the authorities that one consults on the vexed question of referring assume that there is no significance in the vocabulary employed: the Saussurean signified, Mill's connotation and Frege's sense all articulate the same concept (cf. Ducrot and Todorov 1979: 249–51). However, the relation to the referent is very different in all three cases and I want to argue that if we use Frege's terms, which are incomparably the most sophisticated, then it becomes possible to give an account of the text's realism which is more satisfactory than Barthes's and which, suitably modified, allows us also to give an account of the symbolic working of the text which Barthes so brilliantly demonstrates – indeed an account which might be held to avoid reducing the operations of the symbolic to a single crucial term in castration.

Saussure's famous definition of the sign in terms of a signifier and a signified was elaborated in an attempt to capture linguistic identities independently of an appeal to extra-linguistic features. As such they deliberately avoid all reference outside the systematic articulation of sound and sense which constitutes a *langue*. The business of identifying the referent would appear (Saussure says nothing explicit about this problem) simply to follow the

140

organisation of the signified – there is no extra-linguistic reference whatsoever within the Saussurean system.[3] Mill, however, proceeds in the opposite direction. What is given is the variety of the things in the world, these are referred to, named, in the act of denotation, the connotation of a word are those properties which would be specified in a definition of the thing or things named. These two accounts are complementary in so far as they both constitute language and the world as two separate and separable areas – the difference is the epistemological priority accorded to the two realms: for Saussure language determines the world, for Mill the world determines language.

What Frege offers is a way of analysing meaning which avoids this posing of two discrete realms in order to ask questions about the conditions under which we talk of truth or falsity. By holding language and the world within a single theory of meaning, Frege offers the possibility of a theory of meaning which allows an extra-linguistic component without necessarily committing one to realism or representation (though Frege was, in fact, committed to both). If, as analysts of the novel, we interpret Frege, as he wished, in a realist fashion then I think that his theory of meaning provides little illumination. But if we interpret him in anti-realist fashion (as Dummett, following on from Wittgenstein, has suggested) then paradoxically we can give an account of the realist novel which allows it to augment and transform the field of what we can experience directly.[4]

Much of Frege's concern with the problem of meaning arose from the difficulties that confront anyone who wishes to identify meaning and reference (a strategy which has a certain appeal for common sense). Unfortunately this strategy immediately runs into problems about what are going to count as identical meanings. From the very definition of identity, if two objects are identical then everything that is true of one must be true of the other. Thus, if I say that Balzac wrote *Splendeurs et misères d'une courtisane* then it must also be true that the author of *Illusions perdues* wrote *Splendeurs et misères d'une courtisane*. Similarly, to take one of Frege's examples, if the evening star is smaller than the earth then it must be true that the morning star is smaller than the earth because the morning star and the evening star are one and the same object: the planet Venus. But there are certain contexts, which logicians term *opaque*, when one cannot substitute expressions in this way. Thus 'Laura knows that Venus is the evening star' and 'Laura knows that Venus is the morning star' may not have equivalent truth values because everything now depends on Laura's knowledge.

Frege solved this paradox by distinguishing between an expression's reference, i.e. the object, and its sense, the way in which it denotes this object, the specific information that enables you to pick out this object. This distinction solves Frege's problem because what is in question in opaque contexts are the senses, which are different, not the reference, which is the same. It is essential to grasp how different this account is from the Saussurean account of the relation between the signified and the referent where the referent merely falls under the signified. Frege is concerned to give two different criteria for a name (and Frege covers all descriptions when he talks of names) to work. On the one hand there is the sense – the way the name guides you to its object (what Dummett calls its 'semantic role') and, on the other the relation between the name and the bearer (an aspect completely missing from any Saussurean account). It is crucial to Frege's account of meaning that there are two routes to the object – the route through the sense of the referring expression, but also another route, directly to the object, which is non-linguistic. It is how we interpret this *directly* that determines whether we share with Frege a realist view of meaning or whether, while retaining Frege's commitment to an extra-linguistic account, we interpret it in an anti-realist fashion. A realist holds to knowledge-transcendent criteria of truth: the objects of the universe are just given. An anti-realist refuses to consider such questions independently of our ability to assert or verify them. For Frege direct contact will be understood as direct contact with the ultimate constituents of the universe whereas the direct contact for the anti-realist will be within specific practices which will each provide their own specific methods of verification. For the realist, the real is there in the forms that we will come to know, for the anti-realist, the real is there in the forms that we will know it.

To understand how this anti-realist interpretation of Frege enables one to give an illuminating account of the realist novel, one can reflect on Frege's own rather ludicrous comments on literature in his essay on sense and reference. Frege reflects on the Homeric sentence 'Odysseus was set ashore at Ithaca while sound asleep' and confesses himself puzzled by it because we ought to be dissatisfied by the fact that it doesn't have a reference:

> The fact that we concern ourselves at all about the reference of a part of the sentence indicates that we generally recognize and expect a reference for the sentence itself. The thought loses value for us as soon as we recognize that the reference of one of its parts is missing. We are therefore justified in not being satisfied with the sense of a sentence, and in inquiring also as to its reference. But now why do we want every proper name to have not only a sense, but also a reference? Why is the thought not enough for us? Because, and to the extent that, we are concerned with its truth value. This is not always the case. In hearing an epic poem, for instance, apart from the euphony of the language we are interested only in the sense of the sentence and the images and feelings thereby aroused. The question of truth would cause us to abandon aesthetic delight for an attitude of scientific investigation. Hence it is a matter of no concern to us whether the name 'Odysscus', for instance, has reference, so long as we accept the poem as a work of art.   (Frege 1952: 63)

In a revealing footnote to this passage Frege adds that it would be desirable to have a special term for signs having only sense. Frege's position is that if we are concerned with reference then we are concerned with truth-values and truth-values exist independently of our capacity to verify them. Literature thus can have nothing to do with the world of reference, its operations must take place on a different plane of language – a plane so different that ideally one would have special terms for signs only having sense. It is no accident that someone who believes this should choose his examples from Greek epic, for if he had chosen a nineteenth-century realist novel then the problem would have been posed much more acutely. It is not at all clear that we can so clearly dismiss the names of Vautrin and Rastignac as being without reference. It is not simply that these fictional characters are based on the real figures of Vidocq and Thiers, more importantly the senses of those names are so defined in the course of the novel that they enable the reader to make new references in the world, to identify the new men who have come to occupy positions of power in the new spaces, geographical and psychic, offered by the modern city. The realist novel can alter the possibilities of reference, can offer us such different routes to the objects that the objects themselves are transformed. Walter Benjamin makes these possibilities clear when he writes of the way that cinema has liberated us from our urban environments:

> By close-ups of the things around us, by focussing on hidden details of familiar objects, by exploring commonplace milieus under the ingenious guidance of the camera, the film, on the one hand, extends our comprehension of the necessities which rule our lives; on the other hand, it manages to assure us of an immense and unexpected field of action. Our taverns and our metropolitan streets, our offices and furnished rooms, our railroad stations and our factories appeared to have locked us up hopelessly. Then came the film and burst this prison-world asunder by the dynamite of the tenth of a second, so that now, in the midst of its far-flung ruins and debris, we calmly and adventurously go travelling.   (Benjamin 1970: 238)

The novelist who most fully grasped the possibilities of this urban travelling was that assiduous cinema-goer James Joyce who used its techniques for the voyage of Ulysses through the street of Dublin. But the camera's own journey was not simply the result of its technical possibilities but of the novels that had traversed the city streets before it. The point that Benjamin is making can be applied to both film and novel: the realist text allows the possibility of a new sense, a new route to the object, and with this new route the object is changed, transformed. But, and this is an essential part of what Benjamin is saying, that object is not dependent on the cinema or the novel; once we have been shown the route to it, we can verify it independently of the text. The methods of verification cannot be specified in general or in advance; they will find their place in a series of often contradictory practices within which the text finds its reception. What Benjamin forces us to consider is a much more active relation between sense and reference than Frege ever envisaged. (It's worth adding that this is not a purely literary enterprise. It would seem that any serious account of developments in science would have to adopt some version of this thesis.) The anti-realist definition of the role of the extra-discursive allows us to make better sense of some of the claims made for the Balzacian novel. Barthes lumps the whole of the referential code into the figuring by the text of a position of knowledge thus effortlessly occupied by both writer and reader (it might be remembered in passing that this is much more plausible with Sarrasine than it would be with a story wholly set in the Paris of the 1820s). But this strategy simply fails to recognise the social situation of the text; the way in which it opened up a new route into the city. To understand what is at stake in this new access it is not a question of referring to some social content which the text is called to represent but of considering how Balzac's texts enter into a new relation with the audience. It is this new relation which opens up a whole new series of referential possibilities. The relation should not be described in terms of Balzac's imagination but in terms of the new developments in literacy, printing and distribution to which Balzac's writing is, amongst other things, an imaginative response. It was, of course, these developments that Balzac described so brilliantly in *Illusions perdues*, although, for reasons that must be explained, Balzac is unwilling to see these new relations as having any contact with truth which is held to reside within the image of artistic isolation offered by d'Arthez.

These questions of the audience – in terms of the conjunction of new institutional and discursive forms which produced a new reading public (the way in which Balzac's developments as a novelist and developments in journalism through the 1830s are inextricably interlinked would be central to any developed analysis of this conjunction) might relocate the question of realism which simply disappears as an illusion of the text in *S/Z*. If it is no longer possible to see a text as 'representing' a society (if, indeed, these anti-realist arguments dissolve, amongst other things, any notion of a society as an entity which can be considered independently of particular methods of reference and verification), it is still possible to read the text in terms of the presentation of idioms of language and behaviour to a new social grouping. The emphasis in such an account would not be on coherence or comprehensiveness (traditional ways of discussing realism) but on montage, on juxtaposition. To take Barthes's earlier example, the placing of an adulterous intrigue in Rouen, or, in Balzac's case the juxtaposition of the contemporary details of finance, the law and printing with de Rubempré's search for glory.

Barthes's criticism of Flaubert's description of Rouen is that no description of Rouen can ever exhaust its possibilities – it could always be described in some alternative fashion. This is perfectly true but Barthes's formulations seem to ignore the fact that descriptions can always be related to interests and how we choose to describe a particular situation is always a function of why we are describing it. Barthes's objections could be more usefully reformulated in terms of the ways in which the classic realist text ignores any motivation for its descriptions so that they appear unmotivated and final. It is this *finality* within the realist novel which we must now, and most difficultly, address for it is here that classic realism denies its own operations. If we are to understand realism in terms of the construction of new possibilities of referring, why is so much realism presented as though it were simple representation?[5]

Before, however, turning to this disavowal and the problems that it raises, it may be useful to summarise the argument thus far. Any serious account of the novel must both refuse any representational thesis, which always and inevitably ignores the reality of the novel's own existence and operations, and, at the same time, give some account of the extra-discursive element on which the novel gives us an initial purchase. The paradox of my argument is that it is only when we adopt an anti-realist epistemology that we can give a convincing account of realism. This account is not in terms of the representation of a state of affairs but of the process by which the reader is brought to occupy a position from which it is possible to consider new states of affairs, states of affairs which are not dependent upon the novel. The advantage of this account is that it enables us to give an account of two central and common reactions to the novel form: that it enables us to see things anew and that it is possible to have serious disagreement about a novel's realism. On this account such disagreements will be largely about whether we have criteria for recognising these states of affairs independently of the novel's presentation of them. The argument is no longer about whether the novelist represents reality correctly but whether the novelist produces new elements within reality which must then be taken account of. That argument may spread over years and, indeed, decades. One can perhaps follow the strength of a realist text in terms of the various other means of referring that get set up in its wake. In terms of the nineteenth century this would involve considering such things as the relations between novels and the changing law about women and children (law remains our most thorough method of establishing reference) across parliamentary inquiries and other forms of investigation. This position has a very distinct advantage over Frege's account in that it allows for there to be genuine and important disagreements over reference. The anti-realist argument developed here allows the possibility of a theory of reference which would take account of interests.

To fully develop what is here the roughest of sketches would be a very considerable work but the one essential preliminary which can serve as conclusion is an account of the pressures that produce these new positions. For Barthes the fundamental pressure that produces Balzac's text has nothing to do with the new forms of the city and communication in which Balzac's work participates. Instead that pressure is located in an ahistorical symbolic and it is the difficulties of the enactment of the symbolic which sustain and undercut the text in its progress towards Sarrasine's death and the Marquise's refusal of an affair. All questions of realism are thus displaced on to the one referent which it is impossible to name — the phallus understood not as an object but as the signifer of sexual difference. No signified can ever capture this referent for this referent is always significant, always pointing on to another element in the chain of sexual difference. Balzac's whole writing depends on a disavowal of this process but the castrated Zambinella introduces it into the very substance of the novel.

If it is possible to write of this process in Balzac's other novels (cf. MacCabe 1979: 47 – 58), it is the story of Sarrasine set in the past and in another country which liberates Balzac from his normal constraints. It is in terms of the liberation from constraints that Bataille recommends *Sarrasine* in a passage that Barthes quotes as one of the inspirations for his own work (Barthes 1970a). Significantly, Bataille misspells Sarrasine with a *z* and it is this play between *s* and *z* that gives Barthes the title for his analysis. For Barthes the voiced sibilant *z* is the castrating letter *par excellence*, its graphic shape complementing its phonetic qualities. It is this *z* migrating from Zambinella's name to Sarrasine which marks the castration which threatens sexual identity and thus the very basis of representation. Barthes presents this threat ahistorically independently of any of the explicit concerns of the Balzacian text. The only historical element allowed by Barthes is the opposition between the classic and the modern, between the *lisible* and the *scriptible*, between texts wedded to representation and thus anchored in a fixed sexual identity, and a textual and sexual utopianism in which the distinctions which found the category of sexual difference and the possibility of their representation will both be dissolved in a modern text which runs across books and bodies in a ceaseless multiplication of difference which cannot be arrested in a settled identity and a definite form of representation. If such millenarian optimism might be understood in the context of the years when Barthes gave his seminar, that optimism and its implicit valuation of literature, must now be heavily qualified.

The first stage in such a qualification would be to locate this *s* and *z* historically, to understand the question of sexual difference and the enactment of the symbolic in relation to the conditions of the text's production. Such a location is not as difficult as it might first appear for this phonetic play occurs within the history of Balzac's own name. Balzac's family name was originally Balssa and the switch from *s* to *z* was accompanied by the addition of the aristocratic particle *de* (Maurois 1965: 7 – 14). From Balssa to de Balzac. The question of sexual difference is thus tied, as it is in *Illusions perdues* (is Lucien to identify himself through the paternal and plebeian *Chardon* or through the maternal and aristocratic *de Rubempré?*), to the question of social status and it is by examining the status of the author we can begin to delineate a practice of novelistic writing which admitted instead of denying its own operations.

Such a practice would entail that the author took on fully the responsibilities of narration.[6] What those responsibilities are and how they rest on the problematic relation to an unknown audience is sketched brilliantly by Balzac himself in those astonishing and unforgettable scenes in *Illusions perdues* when Lucien writes, to Lousteau's dictation, his reviews of Nathan's novels. These two reviews construct two different versions of reality and the excitement and enthusiasm of the scenes in which they are composed undercut and subvert the simple control of already existing meanings promised by d'Arthez. The elements of such a practice are there in the very existence of *Sarrasine* as a commercial object. The narrator attempts, by telling his story, to gain access to a certain sexual and social identity which would be conferred by the Marquise's acceptance of him as a lover. But the story is not finally related to the Marquise but to an audience that the author does not know and with whom he must engage in the difficult negotiation of what is to count as reality.

I had intended to end there but yesterday's papers by Simon Frith, Ian Chambers and Dick Hebdidge, and indeed the whole conference which I have much enjoyed and which has taught me much, prompts me to add a coda. In the late sixties and early seventies, and under the aegis of those *maîtres* that I invoked by name at the beginning of the paper, we all set out on a theoretical adventure, a ferris wheel of absence and presence, difference and repetition in which we felt that we could grasp both the multifarious realities of the cultural explosions of the sixties and the politics which seemed to issue from that. Our belief in the importance of theory not only came from our situation within the universities, notorious breeding grounds of pomposity and unwarranted self-importance, but also of our infatuation with vanguard parties which foreclosed all the important ethical and political questions that confronted us. This conference seems, under its most optimistic reading, to be moving towards a more just appreciation of theoretical work. In many ways this is a sobering and humbling exercise as we take account of how much other areas of our experience – aesthetic, sexual, institutional – offer, in practices elaborated under a more direct pressure from the real much of what we stumble towards in theory. This is perhaps what Hegel meant when he said that the owl of Minerva takes wing at dusk. Perhaps a more concrete and less classical metaphor would be that theory is always closing the stable door after the horse has bolted. Theory's usefulness may lie in reminding us that this is not a stable to which we can return. My own pleasure in this conference is an increasing conviction that we are now closing one particular door very firmly and we can now, once again, take off after the horse.

Notes

1. I am indebted to Frederick Jameson for indicating to me the importance of this short article.
2. Barthes is evidently talking in terms of a second order of signification. At the level of language, the signifier *barometer* has its appropriate meaning. It is in so far as that linguistic sign is taken up by a literary discourse as a signifier that we can locate the absence of a signified. The relation between literary discourse and language may not, however, be quite as clear-cut as

Barthes's analysis would seem to imply. This, indeed, is the burden of my argument throughout the paper. A further cavil might dispute the 'insignificance' of the barometer in terms of thematic functions.

3. See, for example, Gaukroger 1983: 74. In fact Saussure's discussion of the extra-linguistic is more complicated than the dominant interpretation allows as is argued by Sylvia Adamson in *The Active Voice* (forthcoming).

4. My interpretation of Frege is entirely dependent on Michael Dummett's monumental *Frege: Philosophy of Language*. My reading of Dummett is, in turn, heavily dependent on Stephen Gaukroger's long review of the second edition of the Frege book which appeared in *Oxford Literary Review* VI, 1. On the question of how far these interpretations are faithful to Frege's text, I remain agnostic. What is certain is that Dummett's 'interpretations' are the most interesting account of meaning and reference available. It is also certain that there is constant implicit reference in Dummett's text to the most important philosopher of language in the twentieth century and the most attentive reader of Frege: Ludwig Wittgenstein.

5. It would be in further discussion of this problem that one might distinguish between those infrequent realist works which operate to extend the range of what can be discussed and the vast majority that use the conventions of realism to repeat and reinforce existing patterns of understanding.

6. My understanding of these matters is heavily dependent on the reading of Salman Rushdie's novels.

Bibliography

Adamson, Sylvia (forthcoming) *The Active Voice* (London).
Althusser, Louis (1970) *Reading Capital* (London).
— (1971) 'Ideology and ideological state apparatuses: notes towards an investigation' *Lenin and Philosophy and Other Essays* (London) pp. 121–73.
Arnauld, A. and Lancelot, C. (1969) *Grammaire générale et raisonée* (Paris).
Barthes, Roland (1968) 'L'Effet de réel' *Communications* 11, pp. 84–9.
— (1970 a) *S/Z* (Paris).
— (1970 b) 'L'ancienne rhétorique: aide-mémoire' *Communications* 16, pp. 172–223.
— (1971) *Essais critiques* (Paris).
Bazin, André (1962) *Qu'est-ce que le cinéma* IV (Paris).
Benveniste, Emile (1971) *Problems in General Linguistics* (Miami).
Benjamin, Walter (1970) *Illuminations: Essays and Reflections* (London).
— (1974) 'Left-wing melancholy' *Screen* 15, 2, pp. 28–32.
Bowra, C. M. (1945) *From Virgil to Milton* (London).
Branigan, Edward (1975) 'Formal permutations of the point-of-view shot' *Screen* 16, 3, pp. 54–64.
Brecht, Bertolt (1967) *Gesammelte Werke (werkausgabe)* 20 vols. (Frankfurt-am-Main).
— (1970 a) *Sur le réalisme* (Paris).
— (1970 b) *Sur le cinéma* (Paris).
— (1974) 'Against George Lukacs' *New Left Review* 84, pp. 39–53.
Bynon, Theodora (1977) *Historical Linguistics* (Cambridge).
Curtius, Ernst (1953) *European Literature and the Latin Middle Ages* (London).
Ducrot, Oswald (1968) 'Le structuralisme en linguistique' *Qu'est-ce que le structuralisme?* ed. Francois Wahl (Paris) pp. 13–96.
Ducrot, Oswald and Tzvetan Todorov (1979) *Encycopaedic Dictionary of the Sciences of Language* (Baltimore and London).
Dummett, Michael (1973) *Frege: Philosophy of Language* (London).
Eisenstein, Sergei (1968) *The Film Sense* (London).
Eliot, George (1967) *Middlemarch* (Harmondsworth).
Empson, William (1977) *The Structure of Complex Words* (London).
Flaubert, Gustave (1965) *Trois Contes* (Paris).
Fónagy, I. (1963) *Die Metaphern in der Phonetik* (The Hague).
Fortini, Franco (1974) 'The writer's mandate and the end of anti-fascism' *Screen* 15, 1, pp. 33–70.

Bibliography

Frege, Gottlob (1952) *Translations from the Philosophical Writings of Gottlob Frege* (Oxford).

Fuchs, Catherine and Michel Pêcheux (1975) 'Mises au point et perspectives de l'analyse automatique du discours', *Langages* 37, pp. 7–81.

Gadet, Françoise and Michel Pêcheux (1977) 'Y a-t-il une voie pour la linguistique hors du logicisme et du sociologisme?' *Equivalences*, 2–3, pp. 133–46.

Gaukroger, Stephen (1983) 'Logic, language and literature: the relevance of Frege' *Oxford Literary Review* VI, 1, pp. 68–96.

Haroche, Claudine, Paul Henry and Michel Pêcheux (1977) 'Mises au point et perspectives de l'analyse automatique du discours' *Langages* 37, pp. 7–81.

Harris, Zellig (1952 a) 'Discourse analysis' *Language* 28, pp. 1–30.

— (1952 b) 'Discourse analysis: a sample text' *Language* 28 pp. 474–94.

Heath, Stephen (1975) 'Film and system: terms of analysis' *Screen* 16, 1, pp. 7–77 and 16, 2, pp. 91–113.

Houdebine, Jean-Louis (1976) 'Les Verités de la Palice ou les erreurs de la police? (D'une question obstinement forclose)' *Tel Quel* 67 pp. 87–97.

Huddleston, Rodney (1976) *Introduction to English Transformational Syntax* (London).

Irigaray, Luce (1966) 'Communications linguistique et speculaire' *Cahiers pour l'Analyse* 3, pp. 39–55.

Jakobson, Roman (1960) 'Closing statement: linguistics and poetics' *Style in Language* ed. Thomas Sebeok (Harvard).

— (1963) *Essais de linguistique générale* (Paris).

Jespersen, Otto (1933) *Essentials of English Grammar* (London).

Kristeva, Julia (1974) *La Révolution du langage poétique* (Paris).

Lacan, Jacques (1966) *Ecrits* (Paris).

— (1973) *Le Seminaire XI* (Paris).

Leavis, F.R. (1933) 'James Joyce and the revolution of the word' *Scrutiny* 2, 2, pp. 193–201.

Lukács, Georg (1950) *Studies in European Realism* (London).

Lyons, John (1968) *Introduction to Theoretical Linguistics* (Cambridge).

MacCabe Colin (1979) *James Joyce and the Revolution of the Word* (London).

Marx, Karl and Friedrich Engels (1976) *On Literature and Art* (Moscow).

Maurois, André (1965) *Prométhée ou la vie de Balzac* (Paris).

Miller, Jacques-Alain (1966) 'Avertissement' *Cahiers pour l'Analyse* 1, p. 4.

Mulvey, Laura (1975) 'Visual pleasure and narrative cinema' *Screen* 3, pp. 6–18.

Pêcheux, Michel (1969) *L'Analyse automatique du discours* (Paris).

— (1975) *Les Verités de la Palice* (Paris).

— (1978) 'Are the masses an animate object?' *Linguistic Variation* ed. David Sankoff (New York), pp. 251–66.

— (1982) *Language, Semantics and Ideology* (London).

Safouan, Moustafa (1968) 'De la structure en psychanalyse' *Qu'est-ce que le structuralisme?* ed. Francois Wahl (Paris) pp. 239–98.

Saussure, Ferdinand de (1972) *Cours de linguistique générale*, ed. Tullio de Mauro (Paris).

— (1974) *Course in General Linguistics* (London).

Sidney, Philip (1973) *An Apology for Poetry* ed. G. Shepherd (Manchester).

Strang, Barbara (1968) *Modern English Structure* (London).

Trotter, David (1979) *The Poetry of Abraham Cowley* (London).

Williams, Christopher (1973/4) 'Bazin on neo-realism' *Screen* 14, 4, pp. 61–8.